5-17-07

Electronic Crime

MASTERS SERIES IN CRIMINOLOGY

Series Editor
Henry N. Pontell
School of Social Ecology, University of California, Irvine

White-Collar and Corporate Crime
by Gilbert Geis

Electronic Crime
by Peter Grabosky

Chasing After Street Gangs: A Forty-Year Journey
by Malcolm W. Klein

FORTHCOMING

*Feminist Criminology: Crime, Patriarchy,
and the Control of Women*
by Meda Chesney-Lind

The Great Punishment Experiment
by Todd R. Clear

*Social Support and Crime in America:
A New Criminology*
by Francis T. Cullen

*Social Roots of Crime: Why Some Societies Are
More Violent Than Others*
by Elliott Currie

Developmental and Life Course Theories of Offending
by David P. Farrington

Crimes of Memory
by Elizabeth Loftus

Identity Fraud
by Henry N. Pontell

MASTERS SERIES IN CRIMINOLOGY

Peter Grabosky

Electronic Crime

PEARSON

Prentice Hall

UPPER SADDLE RIVER, NEW JERSEY 07458

Library of Congress Cataloging-in-Publication Data
Grabosky, Peter N.
  Electronic crime / Peter Grabosky.
    p. cm.—(Masters series in criminology)
  Includes bibliographical references and index.
  ISBN 0-13-153461-0
  1. Computer crimes. 2. Computer crimes—History. 3. Computer
  crimes—Prevention. I. Title. II. Series.
  HV6773.G722 2007
  364.16'8—dc22

                                                    2006016914

Editor-in-Chief: Vernon R. Anthony
Marketing Manager: Adam Kloza
Assistant Editor: Mayda Bosco
Editorial Assistant: Jillian Allison
Production Management: GGS Book
  Services
Production Editor: Trish Finley
Production Liaison: Barbara Marttine
  Cappuccio

**Director of Manufacturing
  and Production:** Bruce Johnson
Managing Editor: Mary Carnis
Manufacturing Manager: Ilene Sanford
Manufacturing Buyer: Cathleen Petersen
Senior Design Coordinator: Mary Siener
Interior Design: Lisa Klausing
Cover Designer: Brian Kane
Printer/Binder: R.R. Donnelley & Sons
  Company

Pearson Prentice Hall™ is a trademark of Pearson Education, Inc.
Pearson® is a registered trademark of Pearson plc
Prentice Hall® is a registered trademark of Pearson Education, Inc.

Pearson Education LTD
Pearson Education Singapore, Pte. Ltd
Pearson Education, Canada, Ltd
Pearson Education—Japan
Pearson Education Australia PTY, Limited
Pearson Education North Asia Ltd
Pearson Educación de Mexico, S.A. de C.V.
Pearson Education Malaysia, Pte. Ltd

10 9 8 7 6 5 4 3 2 1
ISBN 0-13-153461-0

To my teachers

CONTENTS

Acknowledgments   ix

CHAPTER 1   Introduction   1

CHAPTER 2   A Brief History of Electronic Crime   5

CHAPTER 3   A Typology of Computer Crime   11

CHAPTER 4   Electronic Crime Explained   43

CHAPTER 5   Incidence, Prevalence, Distribution, and Impacts   49

CHAPTER 6   Trends in Cybercrime   57

CHAPTER 7   Investigation, Prosecution, and Sentencing   69

CHAPTER 8   Conclusion: The Future of Electronic Crime
                  and Its Control   91

Appendix: Useful Websites Relating to Electronic Crime   109

References   111

Index   117

ACKNOWLEDGMENTS

Authors often incur debts in the course of writing books, and this one is no exception. I first began working in the area of computer-related crime in 1995 at the Australian Institute of Criminology. I am grateful to Adam Graycar, who was then the Director, for encouraging me to work in the area and for supporting my work over the following six years. I was joined there at the end of 1995 by Dr. Russell Smith, and since then we have coauthored three books and a number of articles. He has been a great collaborator.

Another collaborator to whom I am indebted is Dr. Gregor Urbas of the Australian National University, coauthor, with Russell Smith and myself, of *Cybercriminals on Trial*. Greg helped lead me into the arcane law of cybercrime jurisdiction.

I am also indebted to Professor Roderic Broadhurst, most recently of the Queensland University of Technology, whose substantial entrepreneurial skills under the auspices of the University of Hong Kong Centre of Criminology produced two Asia Cybercrime Summits in 2001 and 2003, respectively. It was a privilege for me to have participated in both of these, which resulted in a coedited volume, *Cybercrime: The Challenge in Asia*.

I wish also to thank my former Ph.D. student, and more recently my collaborator, Sascha Walkley, for her insights on theories of trust and cybercrime.

Other colleagues from whom I have learned a great deal include Susan Brenner, Dorothy Denning, Donald Piragoff, David Wall, Bill Tafoya, Hedi Nasheri, Yaman Akdeniz, Eugene Spafford, and Jackie Schneider. Des Berwick of the Australasian Centre for Policing Research, one of the pioneers of cybercrime control, both in policy and in practice, also helped show me the way. Michael Stohl first taught me about terrorism longer ago than either of us care to remember and much more recently taught me about cyberterrorism. Nikos Passas encouraged me to pursue additional matters prosecutorial.

The United Nations Asia and Far East Institute for the Prevention of Crime and the Treatment of Offenders (UNAFEI) hosted two workshops in preparation for the Tenth United Nations Congress on the Prevention of Crime and the Treatment of Offenders and produced a workshop on computer crime at the Congress. All of these were great learning experiences, and I am grateful to participants in these events and to successive Directors of UNAFEI, Toichi Fujiwara, Mikinao Kitada, and Masahiro Tauchi, for their hospitality.

Five years later, the Korean Institute of Criminology (KIC) hosted preparatory meetings for the Eleventh United Nations Congress and produced a workshop. Again, it was my privilege to participate in these events, and I thank KIC President Lee, Tae Hoon for involving me in the process.

Over the years, officers of the Computer Crime and Intellectual Property Section of the U.S. Department of Justice, the Australian High Tech Crime Centre hosted by the Australian Federal Police, and the Canadian Ministry of Justice have all shared valuable insights with me.

I am indebted to the Regulatory Institutions Network of the Australian National University and to its Founding Father, John Braithwaite, for providing a splendid intellectual environment in which to write this book. Finally, I am also most grateful to the Series Editor, Henry Pontell of the University of California, Irvine, whose kind invitation to contribute, and friendly encouragement to finish the manuscript, made it all happen.

All of the above have been my teachers, and I gratefully dedicate this book to them.

1 | INTRODUCTION

Most people born after 1990 will not fully appreciate how profoundly the advent of digital technology and the interface of computing and communications have changed our lives. New technologies have dramatically enhanced the capacities of ordinary citizens. In years past, it was often said that freedom of the press belongs to the person who owns one. The ability to communicate directly with the public was limited to media barons and those influential citizens to whom media barons would give voice. Today, nearly anyone can have a website, accessible to the world. It is now possible for ordinary individuals to communicate instantaneously with millions of people, at negligible cost.

Such mundane tasks as research have been revolutionized by digital technology. Rather than leafing manually through printed periodical indexes or library card catalogs, one can conduct electronic searches of databases and, in some cases, download entire articles in seconds.

Of course, these enhanced capacities may be used for good and bad purposes. Digital technology provides both adults and young people with the facility to inflict unprecedented harm. Teenagers have succeeded in manipulating the price of shares on stock exchanges, shutting down air traffic control systems, disrupting large retail enterprises, penetrating the files of military bases, and plucking pirated term papers out of cyberspace. None of this would have been possible before 1980.

This book provides an introductory overview of electronic crime and the means for its control. The term "electronic crime" is a label of convenience and refers to a wide range of crimes committed with the aid of digital technology. The terms "computer crime," "computer-related crime," and "cybercrime" will be used interchangeably throughout the book. Strictly speaking, cybercrime refers to criminal activities involving the networked environment based on the Internet and/or World Wide Web. But we will use it to refer to offenses involving stand-alone computers as well.

One of the most striking aspects of crime in the digital age is its global reach. The phrase "cyberspace knows no boundaries" has become a trite expression. To an unprecedented degree, offenses may be committed by perpetrators on one side of the world against victims or targets physically located on the other side of the world. This, as we shall see, poses profound problems for law enforcement and prosecution authorities.

Nevertheless, there are many aspects of cybercrime that are in principle no different from events on the ground, in terrestrial space, or, in the words of one prosecutor, in "the meat world."

Chapters 2 and 3 will provide a brief history of electronic crime and will describe the various offenses that can involve digital technology. An understanding of electronic crime will then be developed in Chapter 4 by looking at it through the lens of routine activity theory, a simple, but powerful type of analysis that can be applied to all kinds of crime. Chapter 5 will wrestle with the vexing problem of computer

HOW DOES ONE COME TO BE A SCHOLAR OF CYBERCRIME?

I spent most of my career at the Australian Institute of Criminology, moving back and forth between the areas of traditional white-collar crime and violence. One day the Institute's Director came in with a newspaper advertisement, in which Telecom Australia (now Telstra), in those days the national telephone company, was soliciting applications for grants for research into the social implications of telecommunications. Aside from some work on illegal telephone tapping by police, this was *terra incognita* for me. Moreover, I was not a technology buff. I told him as much, but he encouraged me to go ahead in any event. I drafted a proposal to map the various kinds of crime that could be committed with or against computer and communications systems. I was awarded the grant and soon embarked on the research that was to become the piece *Crime in the Digital Age*, co-authored with my colleague Russell Smith.

crime statistics; at the risk of revealing its conclusions, the reader is hereby warned that computer crime is very difficult to measure. The wider social and economic impact of electronic crime is also noted in this chapter, and the reader will learn that digital technology enhances the capacity of both the citizen *and* the state. Next, Chapter 6, on trends in cybercrime, will review some of the most recent developments in the modus operandi of electronic criminals. Chapter 7 will look at issues as cybercrime cases proceed through the criminal justice system, including the stages of investigation, prosecution, and sentencing. The concluding chapter, Chapter 8, will set out some basic principles and strategies for the prevention and control of cybercrime. Finally, both the References and the Appendix contain a number of useful sources that the reader may wish to consult to further his or her knowledge of electronic crime and its control.

ELECTRONIC OFFENDING

Even a glance at historical developments in high-technology crime reveals that every new technology and every new application of that technology are accompanied by criminal opportunities that are quickly exploited. For example, the development of the telegraph in the nineteenth century invited interception of telegraphic communications and transmission of deceptive information. The invention of the telephone was soon followed by its use in furtherance of criminal conspiracies. By the 1970s, telecommunications technology enabled one to whistle into a telephone and obtain a connection, a practice colloquially known as "phreaking." Others, relying on more traditional forms of access, used the telephone to commit various forms of telemarketing fraud.

The advent of high-speed data processing technology in the late 1960s ushered in a new era in crime. Parker (1976), one of the first to write on the criminal applications of information technology, described how computers became the new tool of embezzlers and showed how programmers were able to falsify input and output data for personal financial advantage. Information systems lent themselves to corporate fraud as well. Parker's discussion of the Equity Funding scandal described how the assets of the company were artificially inflated by electronically creating 64,000 fictitious insurance policies.

The new technologies of data processing were ideally suited to high-volume, low-value crimes. Vaughan (1983) described how a large pharmacy chain used a computer-generated double-billing scheme to overcharge governments for health insurance reimbursements.

The development of the Internet beginning in the 1960s and its widespread use beginning in the early 1990s brought about a revolution in high-tech crime. The advent of the personal computer in the early 1980s significantly empowered individual users, for better and for worse. Unauthorized access to computer systems became something of a sport, and some of the more prominent hackers acquired folk-hero status within their subculture. Authorities in the United States were not amused, however, and began to respond forcefully with enforcement and prosecution. The spirit of the times is captured nicely in Bruce Sterling's (1992) book *The Hacker Crackdown*.

The Internet lent itself to quick and efficient communications among users, but was also vulnerable to misuse. The term "hacker" was initially coined to refer to individuals who would obtain unauthorized access to computer systems and then either harmlessly explore them or effect programming improvements. The term "cracker" was applied to individuals of a more malicious bent—those who would use their unauthorized access for destructive purposes, altering or erasing data. In time, the term "cracker" fell into disuse, with the term "hacker" embracing uninvited guests regardless of motive.

A landmark date in the history of computer crime was November 2, 1988, when a graduate student in computer science at Cornell University named Robert Morris wrote a computer program designed to reproduce itself across the Internet. What started out as an intellectual exercise, intended to estimate the size of the Internet, went terribly wrong. He was in other respects a very competent programmer, and the "worm" spread with great rapidity, overloading systems and bringing the Internet to the electronic equivalent of a grinding halt.

More recent developments in the history of computer crime include the increasing sophistication of viruses, the use of digital technology in the production and dissemination of child pornography, and the application of electronics to theft in its various forms (Grabosky, Smith, and Dempsey 2001).

ELECTRONIC CRIME LEGISLATION

Technology tends to develop faster than the law, and the growth of digital technology has inspired legislative efforts to catch up. Although nations differ in terms of technological development and legislative agility, it is possible to identify six historical waves of computer crime legislation (Sieber 1998).

The first, which related to issues of privacy, began in the 1970s. Recognizing that developments in information storage and retrieval were beginning to provide governments with unprecedented capacity to collect, store, and analyze vast quantities of information about individuals, Sweden and other Western democracies moved to enact privacy protection legislation.

The second wave arose in the 1980s, when it became apparent that unauthorized manipulation of computer functions could cause significant economic loss. Legislatures in advanced industrial societies began to prohibit such behavior as unauthorized access to a computer and damage to computer data.

As the software and entertainment industries began to recognize the threat posed by unauthorized copying of their products, they persuaded sympathetic governments to expand existing regimes of intellectual property protection. This represented the third wave.

The fourth wave identified by Sieber related to dissemination of offensive content such as pornography, hate speech, and defamation over the Internet. This wave was very uneven because of the wide variation across nations in the type of conduct that they find sufficiently objectionable to proscribe by law. Even in regard to child pornography, the type of content where there is the greatest agreement regarding prohibition, legislation differs regarding the definition of a child, the definition of pornography, and whether a "virtual" image that has been digitally created (rather than depicting an actual human subject) should be illegal.

The fifth wave of computer crime legislation involved the law of criminal procedure. This tended to focus on procedures for searching and seizing electronically stored evidence and the responsibilities of telecommunications carriers and service providers to assist law enforcement. The development of computer networks brought new challenges in terms of the appropriate measures for the conduct of searches in networked environments that might extend across jurisdictional boundaries.

A sixth wave of legislation relates to security law—specifically, the law relating to surveillance, search, and seizure in the shadow of terrorism. The USA PATRIOT Act (Public Law 107-56), with its provisions for expanded powers of telecommunications interception, is illustrative.

The digital age is a moveable feast, however. Developments in both cybercrime and efforts to control it will undoubtedly continue. This will primarily entail further developments in one or more of the "waves" observed above. In 2003, for example, unsolicited commercial e-mail, colloquially termed "spam," became an increasingly troublesome issue. A number of jurisdictions sought to respond to the problem by prohibiting the sending of such communications (McCusker 2005). The basic issue, that of content regulation, is one with which authorities are already familiar.

It is all but certain that the continued diversification of cybercrime will lead to new legal responses (or at the least the continuing modification of old ones) in order to confront new challenges. The key is to develop legislation that will control undesirable conduct, while allowing legitimate political expression and commercial activity to flourish.

3 | A TYPOLOGY OF COMPUTER CRIME

CATEGORIES OF COMPUTER CRIME

Computer crimes come in a variety of forms, and there is no standard way of categorizing them. As we will see, a single computer crime may actually entail a number of distinct offenses. And some categories are comprised of a diverse range of activities.

One approach is to differentiate those crimes in which the computer is

1. The *instrument* used to commit the offense,
2. The *target* of the offense, or
3. *Incidental* to the offense.

This is a useful, if imperfect, categorization. As will soon become apparent, offenses in which computers are *instruments* and those in which computers are *targets* can overlap a great deal.

Another means of categorizing computer crime is to differentiate between "old" or conventional crimes that are committed with new technology and "new" crimes that are committed with new technology.

ELECTRONIC CRIME TERMS

Hacking: Obtaining unauthorized access to a computer.

Distributed Denial-of-Service Attack: An individual (usually a hacker) gains remote access to a number of computers and directs them against a target (usually a computer system belonging to a government or large commercial entity). By overloading the target computer, the attack impedes legitimate access and may render the system inoperable.

Spam: Unsolicited electronic mail, often transmitted in large volume, whether for legitimate commercial purposes or in furtherance of fraud.

Phishing: Transmitting a form of spam containing links to web pages that appear to be legitimate commercial sites. They are designed to fool users into submitting personal, financial, or password data. Clicking on the link may also lead to infection of one's computer by a virus or may allow access to one's computer by a hacker (Krone 2005a).

Virus: A computer program that may spread from computer to computer, as files containing the program are opened, using up available memory and degrading the "infected" systems and their networked computers.

Worm: A computer program that reproduces itself and spreads through a network, using up available memory. It differs from a virus in that it does not require human intervention (such as the opening of a file) in order to spread.

Extortion, demanding something of value accompanied by a threat of harm in the event of noncompliance, is an ancient practice. Today, however, extortion threats can be communicated electronically over long distances and extortion payments made by means of electronic funds transfer (Grabosky, Smith, and Dempsey 2001, chap. 3). Similarly, the production and dissemination of illicit images of children predated the advent of conventional photography. It remained

TOOLS OF ELECTRONIC CRIME

Network Scanning Programs: Programs designed to identify networked computers and operating systems that might be vulnerable to attack.

Password Crackers: Programs that generate dictionary words or common passwords that might be used to gain unauthorized access to a computer.

Malicious Code: Computer programs designed to cause damage to a computer or system: worms or viruses.

Key Loggers: Applications inserted directly on a computer, or installed remotely, that record the user's every keystroke.

Trojan Horse: A malicious program disguised as legitimate software that, when transmitted to an unsuspecting recipient, may impede the functioning of the target computer system and may even facilitate unauthorized access to, and control over, that computer or installation of a key logger.

Rootkit: A series of programs that hide evidence of an intrusion or the existence of a Trojan.

Bot (abbreviation of robot): A computer program that runs automatically. Some bots have beneficial uses, but others may be employed to gain unauthorized control over a target's computer or to transmit spam.

Encryption: The process of mathematically transforming digital information so that it is unintelligible to anyone other than a person in possession of an algorithm or "key" that will permit the data to be converted to their original state.

Steganography: The process of hiding the existence of information (such as text) by concealing it within other information (such as an image).

Spoofing: Intentionally misrepresenting sender name and address information to make it appear that a message originated from someone else.

Anonymous E-mail: Concealing information that would identify the originator of a message (Gordon, Hosmer, Siedsma, and Rebovich 2002).

labor intensive until the digital age, when technology enabled instantaneous creation, reproduction, and dissemination of images without having to worry about film development and hand-to-hand transfer (Grant, David, and Grabosky 2001). Stalking, too, is an old crime. The offenses of watching and besetting and of criminally harassing date back at least to the rise of the trade union movement, when striking workers were prevented from behaving in a menacing manner toward strikebreakers. Today, digital technology enables the transmission of persistent, unwanted harassing communications from the comfort of one's home.

"New" crimes committed with novel technologies tend to involve unauthorized access to and interference with information systems. The most dramatic manifestations include denial-of-service attacks and the dissemination of malicious code. Before considering these crimes, let us first turn our attention to where many different kinds of computer offenses begin, with hacking.

HACKING

The term "hacking" refers generally to gaining unauthorized access to a computer or a computer system. For some, this is an end in itself. For others, it is the predicate to more serious offending; many of the offenses described below begin with a hack. Most computer systems require some kind of password or access code in order to log on. This can sometimes be determined by guesswork. Some people use their own name or nickname; the term "guest" or "visitor" is not uncommon. Passwords can also be obtained through physical investigation. A person's password might be written on a "Post-It" affixed to the computer monitor. Alternatively, access information may be found by inspecting trash (colloquially referred to as "dumpster diving"). In addition, passwords may be obtained by taking a knowledgeable person into one's confidence (sometimes called "social engineering"). Automated hacker tools, such as password guessing programs and other software that probes for vulnerabilities that may allow for remote access to a computer, are available on the World Wide Web.

In the days before the takeoff of electronic commerce, when businesses, universities, and governments were less reliant on information technology, hacking was regarded with a degree of tolerance. Law enforcement agencies were not always interested in those few cases that were drawn to their attention.

One of the more celebrated early examples of hacking was described in a book entitled *The Cuckoo's Egg*, by Clifford Stoll (1989). Stoll, an astronomer at Lawrence Berkeley Laboratories, was asked to rectify a small anomaly in the accounts of the lab's computer center. He discovered that someone had gained unauthorized access to the lab's computer system and was using this to gain further unauthorized access to other systems around the country. Stoll's book relates one of the first (and best) detective stories in the annals of cybercrime, and the entire story is too good merely to summarize here. A firsthand reading of Stoll's book is essential.

As the vulnerability of information systems and the institutions dependent on them became increasingly apparent, hackers began to achieve wider recognition for their technical exploits. Regarded by some as harmless mischief makers and by others as a serious criminal threat, hackers began to achieve a kind of celebrity status. Many thrived on notoriety and adopted flamboyant nicknames or "handles" by which they identified themselves. A twenty-one-year-old university student in Argentina, Julio Cesar Ardita, obtained access to a system at Harvard University and used it to break into the system of the U.S. Naval Command, Control and Ocean Surveillance Center (NCCOSC).

He then installed "sniffer" programs to capture the identification details and passwords of legitimate users. He went on to penetrate a number of other governmental, educational, and commercial computer systems.[1] Ardita called himself "Griton" ("Screamer" in Spanish).

In 1994, two young hackers in Britain who called themselves "Datastream Cowboy" and "Kuji" broke into a computer system at a U.S. Air Force base in upstate New York, copied sensitive files, and installed password sniffing devices. They launched further intrusions into other defense systems around the United States and downloaded

---

KEVIN MITNICK

One of the more prominent of the early computer hackers was a Californian named Kevin Mitnick. Regarded by some as a cult hero and by others as a "folk devil," in the 1970s he obtained unauthorized access to telephone systems in the Los Angeles area. In 1981, he was arrested for destroying data over a computer network. In 1989, he was convicted under the Computer Fraud and Abuse Act for theft of software from the Digital Equipment Corporation. Following his release, he continued offending, his notoriety earning him a place on the FBI's Most Wanted List. After a nationwide search, he was rearrested in 1995 and held without bail. In 1999, at the age of thirty-seven, he was sentenced to a total of sixty-eight months in federal prison with three years of supervised release. On January 21, 2000, he was released from prison after serving fifty-nine months and seven days. The conditions of his release were extremely stringent, as noted in Chapter 7. Mitnick is now the principal of an information security consulting firm. He is the subject and the author of a number of books on his own activities and on computer security more generally (Mitnick 2002; Goodell 1996).[2]

large amounts of data. These activities were taken seriously by authorities in the United States and Britain, and the two were arrested. Datastream Cowboy was sixteen years old, Kuji twenty-one (Power 2000, 66–76).

In addition to targeting the information systems of large institutions, hackers sometimes attack each other. A celebrated case involved the "Masters of Deception" and the "Legion of Doom," who, in addition to competing with each other to defeat corporate security measures, sought to infiltrate each other's system (Slatalla and Quittner 1995).

ILLEGAL INTERCEPTION OF COMPUTER-MEDIATED COMMUNICATIONS

The old practice of tapping into telephone lines has been eclipsed by new technologies. Today, computer-mediated communications are vulnerable to interception for a variety of purposes. People may be voyeuristic or may seek to capture sensitive information such as credit card details. They may be engaged in political or economic espionage against foreign states or business competitors (Nasheri 2005). Or they may be mistrustful of a spouse.

Mobile phone technology has further enhanced criminal opportunities. By the end of 2005, there were 195 million cellular subscribers in the United States alone (Richtel 2005). Cellular phones are vulnerable to hacking for a variety of purposes. A successful cell phone hacker may listen in to telephone conversations. It is also possible to make a cell phone serve as a "bug" to record background conversations, even when the phone is not in use. Moreover, the convergence of global positioning technology and cellular telephony now enables the identification of the phone's physical location, at least when it is turned on. This is a boon to stalkers and other criminals, and a potential threat to the privacy of ordinary, law-abiding citizens. The upside is that it is also useful to those concerned about the whereabouts of their children or elderly relatives as well as to law enforcement and security agencies.

The colloquial term for technologies that permit the monitoring of someone else's computer is "spyware." For example, a commercially available program called "loverspy" was concealed within electronic greeting cards. When a recipient opened the card, the program secretly installed itself on his or her computer. This enabled the sender to observe all activities on the recipient's computer, including all keystrokes, all incoming and outgoing e-mails, and all websites visited. It was alleged that this technology was acquired by at least 1,000 individuals and used against over 2,000 victims (U.S. Department of Justice 2005a).

CRIMINAL CONSPIRACIES

Just as other communications media such as the telephone have made it easier for collaborating criminals to coordinate their activities, so, too, has digital technology facilitated communication in furtherance of criminal (including terrorist) conspiracies. Technologies of *encryption* make these communications difficult to access for anyone other than the intended recipient (Denning and Baugh 2000). Encryption is the process of mathematically transforming digital information (scrambling all those 1's and 0's) so that they are unintelligible to anyone other than a person in possession of an algorithm or "key" that will permit the data to be converted to their original state. A similar technology called "steganography" embeds information in an image. What may look like a beautiful mountain landscape may in fact conceal records of illegal drug transactions.

Encryption is both a blessing and a curse. It helps protect communications from the prying eyes of voyeurs, business competitors, or a dictatorial government. It provides a modicum of security for legitimate commercial electronic transactions, without which an online economy cannot flourish. On the other hand, it provides criminal conspirators with a powerful tool for concealing electronic evidence (Denning and Baugh 2000).

Digital communications between criminals (or between would-be criminals) may also take place in public. Schneider (2003) described how chemists use Internet relay chat and newsgroups to exchange information on the manufacture and distribution of synthetic illicit drugs and their precursor chemicals. The use of text messages to organize collective activity has also become common (Rheingold 2002). Not all of this activity is legal. Australia, for example, has seen the use of text messages to make plans for group sexual assaults and race riots (Morton 2004; *New York Times* 2005).

Today, the widespread use of digital technology in everyday life means that many "ordinary" crimes will involve some aspect of high technology. Most business records are electronically stored. Cell phones and personal digital assistants are becoming widespread. Global positioning technology now enables the identification of an individual's movements in time and space. We have reached the stage where many, if not most, crime scenes will contain some element of digital technology.

The Internet also enables prospective offenders to meet prospective victims. Aside from varieties of fraud discussed below, the most prominent use of the Internet for such purposes involves adults seeking to meet minors for indecent purposes. Most typically, pedophiles join chat rooms frequented by younger people, begin an electronic relationship, and then arrange to meet somewhere in the physical world.

A more extreme variation on this theme involved a German man, Armin Meiwes, who advertised on the Internet for a person who wanted to be killed and eaten. A fellow German took up the offer. Despite the apparent consent of the victim, the offender was convicted of manslaughter and sentenced to 8½ years in prison. The government successfully appealed on the grounds that the sentence was too lenient, and the accused was retried. He was convicted in May 2006 and sentenced to life imprisonment.[3]

THEFT OF SERVICES

Those unable or unwilling to pay for telephone or Internet services may acquire these services illegally by gaining unauthorized access to a telephone switchboard or Internet service provider (ISP) account. They may then use these services for everyday purposes or on-sell them for a tidy profit. They may also use them in furtherance of a subsequent crime (much as a bank robber will use a stolen car for a getaway).

There are a variety of ways to access services for purposes of theft (Grabosky, Smith, and Dempsey 2001, chap. 5). The original "phone phreakers" were able to reproduce the 2,600-cycle tone used in the U.S. long-distance telephone system. Hardware devices, originally referred to as "blue boxes," replicated long-distance tones and enabled users to bypass the normal telephone switching process. The advent of the Internet enabled aficionados of the telephone system to compare notes through such media as *Phrack* and *2600: The Hacker Quarterly*.[4] A low-tech alternative to "phreaking" was adopted by those who misrepresented their identity and then subscribed for a service without paying for it. The most extreme "bad debt" customers ran up big bills and then simply disappeared.

Internet services are also vulnerable to theft. In 1995, a twenty-year-old Yale student with the online nickname of "Happy Hardcore" designed a software program that allowed him unlimited free access to AOL by exploiting a weakness in that ISP's billing system. He was eventually charged and convicted in what appears to have been the first successful prosecution for theft of services from an ISP (Duva 1997).

One major conspiracy involved a hacker group known as the "Phone Masters," who in the late 1990s hacked into computer systems belonging to major telephone service providers in the United States and stole long-distance calling card numbers. In 1999, two of the principals were convicted and sentenced to forty-one months and to two years in prison, respectively, and each was ordered to pay $10,000 restitution to the victim corporations, including Sprint, Southwestern Bell, and GTE.

FRAUD

The offense of fraud involves obtaining something of value by means of deception. As such, it is as old as human history. Digital technology has enabled old forms of fraud to be perpetrated with great efficiency.

Sales and Investment Fraud

Digital technology permits immediate communications with millions of people at little or no cost. As such, it is ideally suited for advertising goods and services and for soliciting investments. Digital technology has been a boon to legitimate commerce, providing information in unprecedented quantities to inform markets rapidly and efficiently. But it has also been a boon to crooks and con artists.

One has seen fraudulent investment solicitations for schemes as diverse and bizarre as coconut farming and eel husbandry (Grabosky, Smith, and Dempsey 2001, 88–90). One of the biggest Internet frauds uncovered to date involved six defendants who were convicted of marketing a scheme over the Internet that defrauded some 172 investors of a total of more than $16 million. Victims were offered an opportunity to "lease" $1 million from a European bank upon payment of a $35,000 fee. They were assured that the "leased" funds would be invested and would generate a return of $5 million over a ten-month period. The scheme was entirely fictitious. The two architects of the scheme were sentenced to sixteen years and eight months and to eleven years and three months in prison, respectively, and each was ordered to pay restitution of $16,762,000 (U.S. Department of Justice 2002a).

Fraudulent Ordering of Goods

Using stolen credit card details or employing other skills, it is easy enough to order a product online, have it delivered to a temporary address, and then to make off with the goods. One of the more ambitious examples of such a crime involved the alleged activities of a Romanian hacker who defeated a computer manufacturer's security safeguards and gained access to its online ordering system. He then placed orders for over $10 million worth of computers and related equipment, instructing that they be shipped to confederates at "mail drops" around the United States. He and his confederates had recruited additional individuals, including high school students, to receive the merchandise and then either sell it and send the proceeds to Romania or repackage it and ship it there (U.S. Department of Justice 2004a).

Manipulation of Stock Prices

The Internet has dramatically increased the capacity to spread false rumors about shares traded on stock exchanges. Whether through mass e-mailings or through comments made in Internet chat rooms, rumor, hype, or other forms of misinformation can influence the price of shares. By timing one's buy or sell orders carefully, a criminal investor can make a killing, figuratively speaking.

The advent of "day trading," where individuals are able to make their own trades rather than using the services of a stockbroker, has made it possible to engineer a pattern of transactions that gives the impression of movement in a share price. This can be done by a single person who trades on a number of accounts or by two or more individuals who act in concert. In one celebrated case, a fifteen-year-old New Jersey student purchased stock in thinly traded companies and then, using "multiple fictitious names," posted numerous messages on finance message boards recommending the purchase of these particular stocks. The messages included predictions that stock was about to "take off," would be the "next stock to gain 1,000%," and was "the most undervalued stock ever." After the prices increased, the youth sold his shares at a profit (U.S. Securities and Exchange Commission 2000).

Auction Fraud

The creation of online auctions was accompanied by a variety of deceptive practices on the part of both buyers and sellers. In some cases, sellers received payment, but failed to deliver the goods or delivered inferior substitutes. In others, buyers would take possession of the goods, but fail to pay for them. Another common form of auction fraud is to submit a number of fictitious bids in order to drive up the price of the item on sale. In one case, three defendants who had offered a number of paintings for sale created more than forty fictitious user IDs on eBay using false registration data and then placed a number of fraudulent bids for the paintings, significantly inflating the eventual sale prices (U.S. Department of Justice 2001a).

Unauthorized Funds Transfer

Today, the electronic transfer of funds is common practice in Western industrial societies. It is not surprising therefore that criminals might seek to divert the legitimate transfer of funds or to engineer the transfer of funds from legitimate accounts for their own criminal enrichment. In 1994, a mathematician named Vladimir Levin obtained unauthorized access to Citibank's computer system from his office computer in St. Petersburg, Russia. He arranged for accomplices to open bank accounts in Israel, Finland, and California and then began to transfer funds from legitimate Citibank account holders into the accounts of his coconspirators (Power 2000, 92–102).

Embezzlement

Stealing from the boss is as old as the employment relationship. Bosses can steal from companies (and employees), too, as they have since companies were first created. What was once achievable and conceal-able by means of fancy bookkeeping can now be accomplished with information systems. One employee of a not-for-profit operator of hospitals and clinics in northern California used her computer to obtain access to the company's accounting software. She then issued over one hundred checks to herself and others, resulting in losses of over $875,000.[5]

ATM Fraud

Automatic teller machines (ATMs) are common features in most cities and towns. While some offenders use brute force to defeat ATMs (such as ramming them with motor vehicles), others use more subtle means. Some offenders have constructed dummy ATMs that record a customer's card and personal identification number (PIN) details before indicating that the system is out of order. The details are then available for the manufacture of a counterfeit card and its criminal exploitation on a subsequent occasion, whether for use at a legitimate ATM or for the purchase of goods and services. Rosoff, Pontell, and Tillman (1998, 374) described how two ex-convicts built a home-made ATM, installed it in a shopping mall, and left it there for over two weeks while it collected credit card details. Unobtrusive attachments to legitimate ATMs include cameras, card swipe readers, and transmitters that enable offenders to remotely capture credit card numbers and PINs.

DESTROYING OR DAMAGING DATA

There are many ways in which data can be destroyed or damaged. They can be erased or deleted and may not be recoverable. They can be encrypted and thereby made inaccessible to anyone without access to the mathematical formula (or encryption key) by which they were transformed. They can also be altered in such a manner that it diminishes their value or usefulness.

In 2003, the disgruntled former employee of a large Massachusetts high-technology company logged into the company's server and deleted the source code for the software that he had been working on before his contract was terminated. He sought to cover his tracks by altering the computer logs on the server and by impeding access by legitimate employees who were in a position to survey and rectify the damage. Fortunately for the company, the deleted files had been backed up, and the lost data could be retrieved (U.S. Department of Justice 2004b).

Website Defacement

With the advent of the World Wide Web in the mid-1990s, website defacement became a popular pastime of hackers. In 1996, a Swedish hacker group succeeded in altering the website of the U.S. Central Intelligence Agency so that it read "Welcome to the Central Stupidity Agency" (Neumann 1996). Indeed, this and many other examples of hacked websites are archived on the web.[6]

THEFT OF DATA

The kinds of data that might be attractive to a thief can vary widely, from trade secrets, to classified military information, to almost any information that can be on-sold. Commercial organizations place great value on their mailing lists, and large databases of potential customers' contact details can be worth a great deal of money. An employee of a Florida company that was engaged in the electronic distribution of advertising material obtained unauthorized access to the database of a company that maintained commercial mailing lists and stole over a billion records (U.S. Department of Justice 2005b).

Espionage

Much information relevant to national security is stored in digital form. The use of digital technology to access and copy such material is familiar practice. This is also the case with confidential commercial information. Trade secrets and economic intelligence are also valuable commodities. The competitive nature of world commerce is such that companies face a significant risk of becoming victims of industrial espionage. Competitors—and at times, foreign governments—might seek to acquire strategic economic intelligence, trade secrets, or intellectual property by illegal means (Nasheri 2005). Indeed, for many nations, corporate intelligence collection may be more important than defense intelligence collection.

Theft of Credit Card Details

For obvious reasons, one type of data that is particularly valuable is valid credit card details. Most legitimate e-retailers who accept credit card payments for goods and services go to extraordinary lengths to ensure that the credit card details are secure, and they put in place elaborate systems, including sophisticated encryption systems, to this end.

Wireless technology provided a new opportunity to steal credit card details. In late 2003, three men gained access to the wireless network of a large retail store in Michigan. From there, they accessed the chain's central computer system and the systems of its branches around the United States. They then attempted to install a computer program on the systems of several branch stores to capture the credit card details of local customers. The principal member of the conspiracy entered a plea of guilty and was sentenced to nine years' imprisonment. This was a record for the longest sentence imposed in a U.S. federal court for a hacking offense; the most serious online child pornography offenses have attracted longer terms (U.S. Department of Justice 2004c).

MALICIOUS CODE

A variety of computer crimes may fall under the general description of "interfering with the lawful use" of a computer. This may or may not entail unauthorized access. The most common of these are worms and viruses, known collectively as "malicious code."

The writing of self-replicating computer programs was initially the work of computer systems administrators, diagnosticians, curiosity seekers, and pranksters. In the early days of computing, they were of some utility in assessing system performance. Over time, the writing and release of viruses and worms became increasingly the province of negligent or malicious programmers. Since the mid-1990s, as Internet connectivity has increased in the developed world, the damage that can be inflicted by malicious code has become more apparent. The ILOVEYOU virus, released from the Philippines in 2000, caused severe degradation of systems around the world. Although a suspect was identified, the absence of a law in the Philippines that criminalized the release of a virus meant that the alleged offender was never brought to trial.

Significant epidemics of malicious code occur with numbing regularity; the following are among the most prominent of recent years:

1999
   Melissa
2000
   ILOVEYOU
2001
   Anna Kournikova
   Code Red
   Nimda
2003
   Slammer
   SoBig
   Blaster
2004
   Mydoom
2005
   Zotob

Malicious code of a more modest nature appears so frequently that entire industries have developed to detect and remove them. Indeed, any user of a personal computer who does not have antivirus software installed and regularly updated is at great risk of loss or damage to data.

DENIAL OF SERVICE

For whatever reason, people have sought to shut down, or slow down, computer systems since the earliest days of the digital age. The traditional strategy for denial of service was a coordinated "blitz" of e-mail messages or website hits directed at the target computer or system. A large number of users got together and orchestrated simultaneous activity, which, in sufficient volume, slowed a system down or made it difficult (if not impossible) for legitimate users to obtain access. The colloquial term for this is "mail bombing." During the Kosovo conflict at the end of the 1990s, hackers from Belgrade directed an attack against NATO servers, saturating the system (Denning 2001).

Developments in technology have made denial-of-service attacks less labor intensive. In what is called a "distributed denial-of-service attack," an individual (usually a hacker) gains remote access to a number of computers and directs them against a target (usually a computer system belonging to a government or large commercial entity). By overloading the target computer, the attack impedes legitimate access and may render the system inoperable. A fifteen-year-old Canadian who called himself "Mafiaboy" did just that in 2000. These techniques have been refined with the use of "bots" (short for robots), computer programs that run automatically. Some bots have beneficial uses, but others are employed to gain unauthorized control over a target's computer for this and/or other criminal objectives.

SPAM

The term "spam," taken from an old Monty Python routine, refers generically to unsolicited electronic mail. Spam became a problem, and in many places a crime, around the turn of the twenty-first century, when digital technology enabled ordinary individuals to send mass mailings to millions of people at lightning speed and for a cost of next to nothing. The development of bots allowed purveyors of spam to harness the computing power of others' computer systems, significantly enhancing the volume of unwanted communications. Legitimate or otherwise, unsolicited mass e-mails may cause considerable inconvenience to recipients and may detract from system capacity in any organization. At the extreme, this massive increase in unwanted e-mail traffic detracts from the productivity of large organizations, whose employees spent a considerable portion of "company time" disposing of junk e-mail.

One disgruntled supporter of the Philadelphia Phillies sent hundreds of thousands of e-mails complaining about the team. He was able to "spoof" or fake the originator's address so that the spam message appeared to come from legitimate newspapers such as the *Philadelphia Inquirer* and *Philadelphia Daily News*. Many of the destination addresses were invalid, causing the automatic "return" of the message to the purported originators, disrupting the e-mail systems of the news organizations in question. The offender was identified with the assistance of an ISP in Canada and was sentenced to four years in prison (U.S. Department of Justice 2005c).

While the content of some spam is relatively benign, the use of spam in furtherance of criminal activity has become widespread. Among the more common uses of spam are the dissemination of fraudulent investment solicitations, including variations on the classic Nigerian advance-fee fraud letter; the purported sale of pharmaceuticals (such as Viagra) without prescription; and "phishing," deceptive requests for personal financial details (described below). The logic of spam for such criminal purposes is economic, much as is the case for legitimate commercial advertising. The likelihood of any one recipient of a fraudulent solicitation responding positively is small. But communications received by a million individuals will inspire some takers. It only takes a few gullible people to make a fraudster's day.

A SUSPECT SOLICITATION

(This e-mail message was received by the author on December 20, 2005; readers will note the antispam and fraud alert features of the recipient's e-mail system.)

-Originating-IP: [80.89.177.29]

X-Originating-Email: [chies_2005@hotmail.com]

X-Sender: chies_2005@hotmail.com

Reply-To: chiefmrs_odj@yahoo.com

From: "chiea stell" <chies_2005@hotmail.com>

Bcc:

Subject: Urgent Reply

Date: Tue, 20 Dec 2005 09:07:08 -0500

X-OriginalArrivalTime: 20 Dec 2005 14:07:08.0721 (UTC)
   FILETIME=[AA3B9210:01C6056E]

X-PMX-Version: 4.7.1.128075, Antispam-Engine: 2.1.0.0,
   Anti-spam-Data: 2005.12.20.9 external

X-PerlMx-Spam: Gauge=XXXIIIIIII, Probability=37%, Report=
   'FRAUD_419_X3 1.667, FRAUD_419_X4 1.667, LINES_OF_
   YELLING_3 0.671, __CT 0,
   __CT_TEXT_PLAIN 0, __FRAUD_419_LOC 0, __FRAUD_419_
   MONEY 0,
   __FRAUD_419_REPLY 0, __FRAUD_419_TINHORN 0, __HAS
   _MSGID 0,
   __LINES_OF_YELLING 0, __MIME_TEXT_ONLY 0, __MIME_
   VERSION 0,
   __RCVD_BY_HOTMAIL 0, __SANE_MSGID 0, __STOCK_
   PHRASE_7 0'

X-Spam-Score: * (5)

X-PMX-Spam-Score: # (37%)

Office of the Chief Accountant
Stella Obasanjo Foundation
7, Asukoro Lagos Nigeria

Attention: Sir/Madam,

With due respect, I am Dr. Praise David, the chief accountant to the Nigerian late First Lady, CHIEF MRS. STELLA OBASANJO who died on Sunday 4th October 2005. Just before her death, the sum of US$30Million was mapped out meant for Multi-national Hotel Business abroad. For more details about the first lady visit

http://www.cnn.com/2005/WORLD/africa/10/23/obasanjo.obituary/.

With the help of her only beloved son MUYIWA OBASANJO & the Board of Trustees, we are genuinely looking for trusted foreigner who will assist us to establish this Multi-national Hotel Business abroad. The Hotel will be named after the first lady CHIEF MRS. STELLA OBASANJO (memorial)

Benefits:

1. THE FOREIGNER WILL BE A SHARE HOLDER OF 15% OF TOTAL EARNINGS.

2. THE FOREIGNER WILL BE THE COMPANY'S REPRESENTATIVE ABROAD.

3. THE FOREIGNER IS ENTITLED TO ANY BONUS FROM THE COMPANY.

Regards
Dr Praise David
God Bless you.

(The recipient did not reply. An expression of interest would most likely have elicited a request for a "facilitation fee" or for bank account details and access codes.)

EXTORTION

Extortion in the "meat world" is as old as human civilization. Let us look more specifically for a moment at the offense of cyber-extortion. By this, we mean the use of digital technology to obtain something of value by threatening harm to the victim. Digital technology may be applied to extortion in numerous ways (Grabosky, Smith, and Dempsey 2001, chap. 3).

- The Internet can be used as the medium by which a threat is communicated.
- The victim's information systems may be the target of the extortion threat.
- Where the offense entails blackmail, the Internet may be the medium through which the offensive information is communicated.
- Electronic funds transfer may be used as a means of effecting an extortion payment.
- The Internet and World Wide Web may be used to obtain personal information that may identify or be used against prospective victims.

MONEY LAUNDERING

Concealing the proceeds of crime or concealing legitimately earned income from taxation authorities is referred to as money laundering. The process involves transforming ill-gotten gains ("dirty money") into funds from an apparently legitimate source ("clean money"). Electronic financial transactions are in principle traceable. However, the ability to transfer funds around the world, at the speed of light, through accounts in various jurisdictions that may not have the interest in tracing or the capacity to trace financial transactions makes the identification and interdiction of money laundering difficult.

Online banking provides new opportunities for masking the origin of funds. By recruiting unwitting accomplices (such as students) and seeking their assistance (in return for a fee) in transferring funds offshore, a money launderer may circumvent cash transaction reporting requirements.

The U.S. government has expressed particular concern about the use of online gambling facilities in furtherance of money laundering. (Malcolm 2002). Online casinos provide a variety of financial services to their customers, including credit accounts, facilities for the transmittal of funds, and currency exchange services. They may be located in jurisdictions that do not require record keeping or cash transaction reporting. By transferring ill-gotten gains to a casino, gambling a small amount, and then obtaining repayment of the remaining funds, the apparent source of the funds will be the casino, not the criminal activity that generated the money in the first place.

OFFENSIVE CONTENT

Content of questionable taste or of unquestionably *bad* taste abounds in cyberspace. Many countries have made the possession or dissemination of certain kinds of online content a criminal offense. Perhaps the most familiar form of illegal content in the United States involves sexual images of children. The People's Republic of China objects to content extolling the virtues of Falun Gong or of Taiwanese or Tibetan independence. Islamic countries prohibit a wide variety of erotica and do not tolerate content that they regard as insulting to their religion. Many European countries make it a crime to host or to disseminate neo-Nazi propaganda. The United States and some other countries criminalize online gambling. Almost everyone who has ever accessed the World Wide Web will have encountered, intentionally or otherwise, some offensive content.

The problem with content regulation is that it is very difficult to censor the Internet, which was designed to withstand damage to one or more components. Content originating on the other side of the world is just as accessible as material hosted on a server next door.

Putting a particular site out of commission may work for a while, but sooner or later someone else may come along and start again. Countries may take draconian steps such as insisting that all content be filtered through a governmental server, but this comes at a price: Online access may be more difficult, and legitimate use may be constrained. Countries such as Myanmar and North Korea that actively discourage Internet access by all but a few trusted citizens have placed political control ahead of education and economic development as a national priority.

PIRACY

Digital technology permits perfect reproduction, and speedy and widespread dissemination, of text, images, video, sound, and multimedia combinations. In the early days of the digital age, there were those who claimed that cyberspace was fundamentally different from terrestrial space and that all information should be free. This view was not universally shared, least of all by the software and entertainment industries, whose future depended significantly on the commercialization of digital products. Despite the extension of copyright protection to content that exists in digital form, there were those who sought to copy and distribute intellectual property free of charge, almost as an act of rebellion. More recently, as professional and amateur criminals became aware that there was a great deal of money to be made in pirated content, piracy, too, became commercialized.

An illegal software piracy group called Drink or Die had members in a number of countries around the world. It was estimated to have distributed more than $50 million in illegally produced software in the three years prior to its disruption by an investigation culminating in simultaneous raids in December 2001.[7]

FORGERY

Scanning technology has become so refined that perfect copies of documents can be easily made. These can range from identity documents such as birth certificates to currency. Designer labels can also be copied with uncanny accuracy. Some forgeries are less than perfect, however. One aspiring forger who sought to reproduce currency at home using a basic scanner and Page Maker® software was convicted of counterfeiting (*United States v. Godman,* 223 F.3d 320 (6th Cir. 2000)). Websites can also be counterfeited, with uncanny accuracy, for a variety of purposes including fraud and protest.

STALKING

Stalking is not unique to the digital age. Persistent, unwanted harassing communications are not new. We have already referred to the offense of "watching and besetting." Obscene telephone calls are as old as telephony. But digital technology certainly increases the capacity of those who would like to direct unwelcome communications against a target (Ogilvie 2000). This can be done repeatedly, at the click of a mouse. Moreover, digital technology can be mobilized to recruit others and involve them in activities against the victim.

In one case, a rejected suitor posted invitations on the Internet under the name of a twenty-eight-year-old woman, the would-be object of his affections, that said she had fantasies of rape and gang rape. He then communicated via e-mail with men who replied to the solicitations and gave out personal information about the woman, including her address, her telephone number, details of her physical appearance, and instructions on how to bypass her home security system. Strange men turned up at her home on six different occasions, and she received many obscene phone calls. While the woman was not physically assaulted, she would not answer the phone, was afraid to leave her home, and lost her job (Miller and Maharaj 1999).

A former university student in California used e-mail to harass five female students, apparently in response to their teasing him about his appearance. He bought information on the Internet about the women using a professor's credit card and then sent 100 messages, including death threats, graphic sexual descriptions, and references to their daily activities (Associated Press 1999).

For some years now, developments in digital technology have permitted exploitation of a backdoor into the operating system of victims' computers. Offenders have been able to insert Trojan horses or other spyware in the computers of their targets, enabling them to monitor their victims' keystrokes and even take control of their computers.

PHISHING

One of the more recent manifestations of online crime is "phishing." This most commonly entails the posting by a spammer of mass e-mails purporting to be from a legitimate source, usually a financial institution. The e-mail message, often embellished with a forgery of the institution's letterhead or linked to a counterfeit webpage, may say that the institution is conducting a security audit and would like to verify the user's account number and access code or PIN. If the user "takes the bait" and reveals the requested information, the offender will then withdraw the funds from the account or use the credit card details to make purchases before the legitimate account holder can take any action.

In another variation of phishing, the e-mail message includes a website link, with an invitation to access it. Clicking on the link may expose one's computer to a virus or grant access to an intruder who may then use one's computer for a variety of criminal activities. This is a good reason why one should not respond to, or even open, an e-mail that appears to be from a suspicious sender.

TERRORISM

One of the more prominent issues of our time is the threat of terrorism. The term "cyberterrorism" has been used rather loosely to refer to the application of digital technology to terrorist activity. Denning (2001, 10) offers one way of conceptualizing cyberterrorism: "unlawful attacks against computers, networks and the information stored therein when done to intimidate or coerce a government or its people in furtherance of political or social objectives."

For some years now, thoughtful people in industrialized societies have been alert to the threat of attacks against what we call "critical infrastructure." These communications, electric power, air traffic control, and financial systems all depend on software and are vulnerable to disruption. The annals of cybercrime contain examples of successful attacks against air traffic control systems, sewage treatment facilities, and large electronic retailers, as well as the occasional mail bombing of governmental servers and defacement of governmental websites. But none of these meets Denning's definition.

Although the "electronic Pearl Harbor" scenario may be remote, there are a number of ways in which digital technology can be used in furtherance of, or complementary to, terrorist activity. Digital technology, of course, may be used for the remote detonation of explosive devices. And while Denning may be correct in asserting that terrorists continue to prefer truck bombs to logic bombs, the use of a cyber-attack to complement or enhance a terrestrial attack should not be discounted. Imagine, for example, if an attack on the scale of 9/11 were accompanied by a takedown of the telephone and electric power systems in the target metropolitan area.

CRIMINAL ATTACKS ON CRITICAL INFRASTRUCTURE

In March of 1997, a computer hacker disabled a telephone company computer serving the local airport in Worcester, Massachusetts. This disrupted services to the airport's control tower for a period of six hours. The attack also shut down a circuit that enabled aircraft to activate the airport runway lights on approach. NYNEX (later Bell Atlantic) notified the U.S. Secret Service, which shared responsibility for computer crime investigation with a number of federal agencies. Investigations led to a juvenile who had also disrupted local telephone service and had accessed the prescription records of a local pharmacist. The case was the first federal prosecution of a juvenile for a computer crime. The juvenile pleaded guilty and was sentenced to two years' probation and 250 hours of community service, was required to pay restitution to the telephone company, and was prohibited from possessing a modem or other means for remotely accessing a computer or network.[8]

In February 2000, a person obtained remote access to a number of computers at U.S. universities and then directed their computing power against a number of prominent e-commerce sites, including CNN, Yahoo, Amazon.com, eBay, and Dell. The targets were flooded with data, preventing their normal operation. Some were shut down completely; others were seriously degraded to the extent that it took users minutes to access their web pages. The attacks were of particular concern in that they threatened public confidence in the security of electronic commerce, then in its relatively early stages. It became apparent that the attack had originated in Canada. The Royal Canadian Mounted Police arrested a fifteen-year-old Canadian boy who had boasted of various exploits over the Internet. "Mafiaboy," as he called himself, was sentenced to eight months' detention in a youth training center.[9]

In March 2000, a failure at a sewerage pumping station operated by Maroochy Shire in Queensland, Australia, caused the discharge of 264,000 gallons of raw sewage onto the grounds of a five-star resort and local parks. A forty-nine-year-old employee of the company that installed the system, said to have been an unsuccessful applicant for a job with the shire, was found with a laptop computer, a remote telemetry system, and a two-way radio and antennae. He was alleged to have made at least forty-six attempts to gain control of the system. He was sentenced to two years' imprisonment (*R. v. Boden*, [2002] QCA 164).[10]

On September 20, 2001, computer systems at the Port of Houston, Texas, the eighth largest shipping port in the world, were the target of what appeared to be a denial-of-service attack. The port's web service became unavailable to shipping companies, piloting and mooring services, and others essential to maintaining port operations. The port may not have been targeted intentionally, as the attack appears to have been aimed at a chat room user who was perceived to have offended the girlfriend of the alleged perpetrator. The attack traveled through various intermediary computers before reaching the target computer; one of these was at the Port of Houston. The accused, a resident of England, denied any knowledge of the attack, claiming that the evidence was planted on his computer by unknown hackers who had used a Trojan horse program. The jury accepted the defense and the accused was acquitted (Brenner, Carrier, and Henninger 2004).

Technology as a Means to Facilitate Terrorism

Of course, digital technology can enhance the efficiency of any organization, legitimate or otherwise, that makes use of it. For example, it lends itself nicely to the following terrorist applications (Thomas 2003):

• *Intelligence:* Terrorists may seek to acquire open-source (publicly available) intelligence on an adversary or collect classified information by hacking into the adversary's computer systems.

• *Communications:* Members of terrorist groups may send and receive messages, often concealing their content through encryption and steganography (concealing messages within images). The nature of the Internet and World Wide Web is ideally suited to communications across widely dispersed elements of a network.

- *Propaganda:* Terrorist groups may communicate directly to a general worldwide audience or to specialist target audiences, bypassing journalistic editing and government censorship. This may include inflammatory hate speech intended to legitimize violence against specified adversaries. A newscast alleged to have been produced by al Qaeda was published on the Internet in September 2005.[11]

- *Psychological Warfare:* The Internet may be used as a means of tactical deception by terrorist organizations. By generating anomalous patterns of traffic, they can give the erroneous impression that an operation may be imminent. The fabrication of "chatter" may distract law enforcement and intelligence services from true terrorist activity.

Another form of psychological warfare can involve general or specific threats or displays of force. Webcasts of hostages, and even hostage executions and bombings, can reach the world.[12] These may be coupled with threats against nationals of specific countries who may be identified with causes anathema to the terrorist organization.

- *Fund-Raising and Recruitment:* Terrorist groups may raise funds through charity and other front organizations, or they may actively seek to recruit new members. The cities of Europe house many young, resentful Muslim males. Some of them may well be attracted to militant causes. Webcasts that celebrate martyrdom may be particularly useful in attracting the attention of prospective suicide bombers.

- *Training:* Terrorist groups may use the Internet and the web to teach attack techniques and skills. For example, in 2005 an alleged al Qaeda training manual (in English translation), seized during a raid on suspect premises in the United Kingdom, was posted for a time on the website of the U.S. Department of Justice.[13]

ENDNOTES

1. http://www.wasc.noaa.gov/wrso/security_guide/hacking.htm (visited July 6, 2006).

2. http://www.usdoj.gov/criminal/cybercrime/mitnick.htm; http://www.kevinmitnick.com/index.php (visited June 1, 2006).

3. http://news.bbc.co.uk/1/hi/world/europe/4752797.stm (visited June 1, 2006).

4. http://www.phrack.org; http://www.2600.com.

5. http://www.usdoj.gov/criminal/cybercrime/sabathiaPlea.htm (visited July 6, 2006).

6. See http://www.2600.com/hacked_pages/old_archives.html (visited July 6, 2006).

7. http://www.usdoj.gov/criminal/cybercrime/ob/OBMain.htm (visited July 6, 2006).

8. http://www.usdoj.gov/criminal/cybercrime/juvenilepld.htm (visited July 6, 2006).

9. http://cbc.ca/cgi-bin/templates/view.cgi?/news/2001/01/18/mafiaboy010118 (visited July 6, 2006).

10. http://permanent.access.gpo.gov/websites/unt/nipc/www.nipc.gov/publications/highlights/2002/highlight02-03.htm (visited July 6, 2006).

11. http://abcnews.go.com/WNT/Investigation/story?id=1164648&WNT= true (visited June 1, 2006).

12. http://siteinstitute.org/bin/multimedia.cgi?Category=video&Subcategory=0&sort=newest&Rank=1&Mode=List (visited June 1, 2006).

13. http://www.usdoj.gov/criminal/cybercrime/s&smanual.2002.htm (visited July 6, 2006); http://www.pbs.org/wgbh/pages/frontline/shows/network/alqaeda/manual.html; http://www.pbs.org/newshour/bb/terrorism/july-dec05/online_8-02.html (visited June 1, 2006).

4 | ELECTRONIC CRIME EXPLAINED

To understand where and why cybercrime occurs, it is helpful to rely on a theoretical framework. One useful perspective is that of routine activity theory (Cohen and Felson 1979). Although developed to explain conventional "street" crime, the theory is sufficiently robust to account for cybercrime as well. Essentially, cybercrime can be explained by the intersection of three factors:

1. A supply of motivated offenders,
2. A supply of suitable targets or prospective victims, and
3. The absence of capable guardians.

Each of these factors must be present in order for a cybercrime to take place. Remove at least one, and a crime will not occur. Unfortunately, this is easier said than done.

MOTIVES

The supply of motivated offenders is a reflection in part of the number of individuals with access to the tools of cybercrime. All else being equal, the more people who are connected to the Internet, the more who are in a position to use the technology for illegal purposes.

To date, in Western industrial societies at least, there has been an exponential growth in the number of people with access to computers. Table 4-1 illustrates the differential take-up of digital technology around the world. Nearly one in every six people around the world has accessed the Internet, but the digital divide remains rather large. For example,

TABLE 4-1 WORLD INTERNET USAGE AND POPULATION STATISTICS

World Regions	Population (2006 Est.)	Population (% of World)	Internet Usage (Latest Data)	% Population (Penetration)	Usage (% of World)
Africa	915,210,928	14.1 %	**23,649,000**	2.6 %	2.3 %
Asia	3,667,774,066	56.4 %	**364,270,713**	9.9 %	35.6 %
Europe	807,289,020	12.4 %	**291,600,898**	36.1 %	28.5 %
Middle East	190,084,161	2.9 %	**18,203,500**	9.6 %	1.8 %
North America	331,473,276	5.1 %	**227,303,680**	68.6 %	22.2 %
Latin America/ Caribbean	553,908,632	8.5 %	**79,962,809**	14.4 %	7.8 %
Oceania/ Australia	33,956,977	0.5 %	**17,872,707**	52.6 %	1.7 %
WORLD TOTAL	6,499,697,060	100.0 %	**1,022,863,307**	15.7 %	100.0 %

Note: (1) Internet usage and world population statistics were updated on March 31, 2006. (2) Demographic (population) numbers are based on data contained in the world-gazetteer website. (3) Internet usage information comes from data published by Nielsen//NetRatings, by the International Telecommunications Union, by local Network Information Centers, and by other reliable sources. (4) For definitions, disclaimer, and navigation help, see the Site Surfing Guide http://www.internetworldstats.com/surfing.htm. (5) Information from this site may be cited, giving due credit and establishing an active link back to www.internetworldstats.com. © Copyright 2006, Miniwatts Marketing Group. All rights reserved.

nearly two-thirds of North Americans, but less than 3 percent of Africans have online access. Asia, with more than half of the world's population, but with less than 10 percent of the persons connected, is poised for dramatic growth in the years ahead, as its economies develop.

Individual motives for specific forms of cybercrime are as varied as the crimes themselves. Moreover, the motivation for a particular cybercrime may be complex, or mixed. Hacking and what might be called cybervandalism are often the work of the curious, the adventurous, or the attention seeking. Many hackers are motivated by curiosity, to see just how far they can venture into cyberspace. Some hackers have spoken of a feeling of exhilaration when obtaining access to a previously secure system. Many of them seek to bask in their own notoriety by boasting of their exploits to peers.

In the case of financial crimes, in cyberspace as in terrestrial space, the motive is usually greed. Lust is reflected by the ubiquity of sexually explicit websites (entirely legal in some jurisdictions, but forbidden in others). Rebellion often underlies efforts to inflict damage on symbols of power, whether the White House, McDonald's, or the Yasukuni Shrine in Tokyo (McNicol 2005). Revenge may be seen in theft or damage inflicted on an institution's information systems by a disgruntled employee or former employee.

The reader will already have noticed that the motives for computer crime outlined above are by no means modern phenomena, unique to the digital age. Greed, lust, power, curiosity, rebellion, revenge, and the desire for celebrity (or notoriety) are as old as recorded human history, and deeply engrained in the human behavioral repertoire. If there is anything new about motivations for cybercrime, it is the desire to master complex systems.

As was the case with the supply of motivated offenders, the supply of targets or prospective victims is a function of the take-up of digital technology. Beyond the exponential increase in the number of individual users, the increasing connectivity of computers and communications and the pervasiveness of computers in Western industrial societies mean that more and more institutions and services depend on digital technology. It has been over a decade since someone observed that "everything depends on software" (Edwards 1995). Institutions of critical infrastructure such as electric power, water supply, telecommunications, air traffic control, and banking are all networked. An increasing volume of commerce occurs online. Most readers will deal with ATMs and online banking rather than with human tellers in bank branches. Books, software, music, and video are all available for purchase electronically. Online auctions such as eBay process millions of transactions daily.

The basic idea is that each new technology, from the Internet, to the World Wide Web, to encryption, to wireless networks, can be exploited for criminal purposes. And each new application, from Internet chat rooms, to electronic funds transfer, to online share trading, to the use of one's credit card for Internet purchases, presents a new opportunity for someone to commit crime.

In the world of terrestrial crime, some targets are more vulnerable than others. The term "target hardening" is used to refer to measures employed to block criminal opportunities. So one sees deadbolts on doors and windows, engine immobilizers on motor vehicles, and bullet-proof glass. The same principles apply in cyberspace, where a variety of technologies have been developed to reduce computer systems' vulnerability to criminal exploitation. These include firewalls, antivirus software, blocking and filtering technologies, encryption, and a variety of access controls from passwords to biometric authentication systems.

The basic challenge of opportunity reduction in cyberspace, as on the ground, is to minimize inconvenience to legitimate users, while maximizing the effort required on the part of criminals. Like much in life, this requires a trade-off. In the earliest days of the Internet, people left their doors unlocked, so to speak; most were not concerned if their "neighbors" came in and wandered around. Today, with significant assets to protect and with many potential criminals lying in wait, you ignore system security at your peril.

GUARDIANS

The third element of routine activity theory and the *sine qua non* of electronic crime is the absence of capable guardians. By this, we mean someone (or something) to "mind the store." The basic function of a guardian is to exercise surveillance over people and places for the purpose of preventing crime or to enable prompt response in the event that a crime is committed. In the terrestrial world, capable guardianship may be exercised by *living people*, such as parents, teachers, and the police officer (or private security guard) on the corner, or by *technological applications*, such as burglar alarms or CCTV cameras in stores, offices, or public places. In cyberspace, parents monitor their children's use of the Internet to ensure that they do not venture into places that would make them vulnerable to victimization or to offending. Employers monitor employees' use of their organization's information systems to guard against electronic misconduct ranging from engaging in sexual harassment, to exposing the system to viruses, to wasting time on the job. Systems administrators keep an eye open for unauthorized access or malicious code that can shut down or seriously degrade the capacity of a computer network. Technological means of capable guardianship in cyberspace are abundant. For example, standard Windows software systematically records websites that have been visited. Intrusion detection programs identify hacking attempts. Encryption technology enables one to conceal information from those for whom it is not intended.

Of course, would-be guardians do not always function the way they should. Parents may be lacking in computer literacy or may be careless in supervising their children. Computer users may be nonchalant about the sites they visit and about the e-mail attachments they open. They may use passwords that are easy to guess, or they may even leave them in plain view. They may fail to install or to update their virus detection software.

In the earliest days of the digital age, people were fairly nonchalant about information security. The Internet was designed as an information commons; people were not terribly concerned about ownership or privacy. Software was designed for user friendliness and ease of interface rather than for security. With the diffusion of digital technology and its application throughout individual and organizational life, things changed. Opportunity reduction and stricter guardianship are becoming more common, and none too soon.

5 | INCIDENCE, PREVALENCE, DISTRIBUTION, AND IMPACTS

Just as terrestrial crime has its "dark figure" (offenses that are not reported to police), so, too, does cybercrime. The reasons for nonreporting are similar. In some instances, the victim or victims may not know that they have experienced a crime. Victims of successful charitable contribution frauds are left feeling good about themselves, not knowing that their "contribution" has gone to a criminal rather than to those truly in need. This can happen in cyberspace as easily as on the ground. In the digital age, we must realize that software is not always perfect and that "glitches" and "bugs" appear from time to time. Whether a malfunction occurs "naturally" or whether it is induced by foul play may not be immediately apparent.

A great deal of cybercrime that *is* recognized as such is relatively trivial. Few users of the Internet have been able to avoid receiving e-mail variations on the classic Nigerian advance-fee fraud letter, asking for assistance in (and offering a commission for) moving a large

There is an Australian saying that if one is seeking an explanation for an adverse event, it is more likely to arise from a mistake than from a conspiracy. This is often the case with computer mishaps. The original "bugs" in computing were real insects. Telephone service in one rural U.S. community was once disrupted, not by a hacker, but by a farmer who unknowingly cut an underground telephone cable while trying to bury a dead cow. I was, on two separate occasions, single-handedly responsible for crashing the computer system at the Australian Institute of Criminology. In both instances, my modus operandi was to leave a space after a comma in an internal e-mail message sent to multiple addressees. This was entirely unintentional, due only to my lack of manual dexterity. The result was that I overloaded the system with messages. The Institute soon upgraded its e-mail system to one that was more robust.

amount of cash. Most recipients of such messages erase them and don't bother to report them to police.

Victims are often inclined to seek a quick remedy, rather than mobilizing the law. When vandals snap my car radio antenna, I replace it. Few recipients of "phishing" spams report them. When I receive a message from a "bank" asking me to confirm my account number and PIN, I erase it. Indeed, on all but one occasion, the "financial institution" seeking my details was one with which I have never held an account.

Even more serious matters may also escape official attention. Large financial institutions that have been defrauded may be reluctant to disclose their victimization, whether terrestrial or electronic. Rather than disclosing their vulnerability (and in the process generating bad publicity), they may be inclined to "swallow" their loss.

Even when electronic crimes are reported to police, they may not be transformed into crime statistics. This, too, may reflect the trivial nature of the offense, especially if there is no immediate loss or damage. Police may also lack the resources and the capacity to deal with computer crime. Some officers of the "old school," who are more comfortable when they are looking angry men in the eye, regard computer forensics as something other than "real police work" (Goodman 1997).

As noted above, with a great deal of computer-related crime, digital technology is only instrumental to, or incidental to, a conventional offense such as fraud, extortion, or drug dealing. When these offenses are counted in police statistics, they are usually classified in accordance with the nature of the substantive offense, not the means by which the offense was committed. So extortion is extortion, whether the threat was communicated in longhand or via e-mail. Whether plans for a drug deal are made over the Internet or records of the deal are stored in digital form is irrelevant to the principal charge. Suffice it to say that a large proportion of computer-related crimes is never enumerated as such.

In contrast to the underestimation of the *incidence* of crime involving digital technology, estimates of the *costs* of computer crime are vulnerable to inflation. In most modern jurisdictions, where law enforcement and prosecutorial resources are finite, the relative seriousness of a crime may determine whether it receives official attention. A victim who values police attention may well place the most generous possible construction on the losses he or she may have sustained at the hands of a cybercriminal.

Unless they choose to conceal their victimization, some industries go to great lengths to estimate their losses. This is especially so when they prefer that governmental authorities place the interests of the industry, and criminal exploitation of these interests, high on the public agenda. The rigor of some estimates may at times be called into question. Industries based in e-commerce may have a vested interest in understating their losses, while others, such as the entertainment industry, will have no such incentive.

At the end of the day, one should approach statistics of cybercrime with extreme caution. At the very least, one should seek to determine the assumptions that underlie various estimates.

STATISTICS

Rather than a perfect and comprehensive picture of computer crime, what we have resembles more a mosaic. It is indicative of general patterns and trends rather than precise enumeration. As an alternative to enumerating offenses coming to police attention, some success in judging the prevalence of computer crime has resulted from surveys. Some are "one-shot" surveys, while others are conducted annually. In some cases, the sampling frames may differ, making year-to-year comparisons risky at best. Each year since 1996, the Computer Security Institute and the FBI's San Francisco office have conducted a survey of U.S. institutions in the public and private sectors (Gordon et al. 2005). These give a rough indication of the experience of these institutions. Consistently since 1999, over 70 percent of institutions have reported experiencing at least one incident per year. The most recent survey found that virus attacks, unauthorized access, and denial of service, in descending order, were the three greatest contributors to an organization's financial loss. Total losses reported by those surveyed ($N = 639$) were $130,104,542.

The Australian Institute of Criminology has compiled one of the best collections of the pieces of the mosaic of cybercrime.[1] Some are based on reports to one agency. The Internet Crime Complaint Center (IC3), for example, publishes regular counts of complaints that it receives.[2] These statistics, of course, represent the awareness and underlying motivation of citizens as much as the incidence of criminal behavior. Online auctions have been the source of most reports since

1997; general online sales, the second most significant source of reports to the IFCC, have given rise to an increasing number of complaints since 1998.

The British Crime Survey (BCS), a nationally representative survey of private households in England and Wales, began sampling citizens to measure the incidence of criminal victimization in 1982. It is arguably the most rigorous survey of criminal victimization conducted by any government. In 2002, for the first time, the BCS included questions related to computer crime (Allen et al. 2005). In that year, 18.2 percent of respondents with an Internet connection at home reported that their computer had been affected by a computer virus in the previous twelve months. Only about a third reported it to anyone, and the police were notified in less than 1 percent of cases. Twelve percent reported having received an e-mail that they regarded as offensive or threatening, and 2.2 percent reported that someone else had gained access to their computers; none of these incidents was reported to police.

The Business Software Alliance estimates that globally, for every two dollars' worth of software purchased legitimately, one dollar's worth is obtained illegally. This amounts to $30 billion per year.[3] It may come as no surprise that those nations with the highest rates of piracy (China, Vietnam, Ukraine, and Indonesia, where more than 90 percent of all software is said to be pirated) are from the developing world, while those with the lowest piracy rates (the United States, New Zealand, Denmark, and Austria, with rates around 20 percent) are among the most affluent.

A 2003 survey of 333 online merchants in North America revealed that revenue loss arising from online credit card fraud was 1.3 percent. Based on the level of business-to-consumer online sales, this was estimated at $1.6 billion for the year.[4]

A survey of public- and private-sector organizations in Australia, modeled to some extent on the U.S. Computer Crime and Security Survey, revealed that one-fifth of respondents had experienced an electronic attack in the past year, a decline from previous surveys (AusCERT 2006). Infections from worms, viruses, and Trojans were the most common form of attack. The report further observed that attacks motivated by financial gain were increasing both in volume and in sophistication.

IMPACTS OF CYBERCRIME

The actual or potential impacts of computer crime are serious indeed. To the extent that people have become dependent on, if not addicted to, digital technology, any disruption or degradation of information systems can be extremely costly. In addition to the extrinsic costs of computer crime, there may be certain intrinsic costs borne by victims as well. While relatively few readers may have felt the fear instilled by a stalker, many, if not most, will have lost a few hours' work as the result of malicious code. The panic of losing data, whether as a result of foul play, system malfunction, or negligence, is a nontrivial experience. Extend this across a large organization or network, and the losses, extrinsic and intrinsic, add up.

Although quantification of computer crime and its financial impact is often fraught with hyperbole and wild speculation, some degree of rigor is being brought to the task.

Calculating costs incurred as the result of such attacks is always risky; the estimated losses to businesses worldwide from the ILOVEYOU virus ranged from just under $1 billion to $15.3 billion in computer downtime and software damage (Beh 2001; Grossman 2000).

There are more insidious costs to be reckoned with. Another consequence of the digital age, of relevance to law-abiding citizens and

COSTS OF CYBERCRIME

- Some estimates of the extent or cost of e-commerce crime are provided by Newman and Clarke (2003).

- The ILOVEYOU virus was estimated to have cost users worldwide at least $950 million, with estimates as high as $6.9 billion for lost data, lost business, lost productivity, and remediation.[5]

- The costs of the Mafiaboy DDOS attacks were estimated at $1.7 billion.[6]

- The person who released the Melissa virus acknowledged in his plea agreement that the virus caused at least $80 million in damage.[7]

cybercriminals alike, is the enormous capacity for surveillance that digital technology places in the hands of governments and private organizations. Ordinary computer users leave their tracks all over cyberspace. It is possible, using data-matching technologies, to build extensive electronic dossiers. Official reactions to cybercrime often entail a greater willingness and ability to compile databases of personal information and to intercept private communications.

ENDNOTES

1. http://www.aic.gov.au/stats/crime/cybercrime.html (visited July 6, 2006).

2. http://www.ic3.gov/media/annualreport/2005.IC3Report.pdf (visited July 6, 2006).

3. Business Software Alliance. 2005. *Second Annual BSA and IDC Global Software Piracy Study.* http://download.microsoft.com/download/F/0/3/F034C5EE-7E49-402A-9D5C-BD81C1D0AF94/IDC-Piracy%20Study.pdf (visited June 1, 2006).

4. CyberSource. 2004. *5th Annual Online Fraud Report: Credit Card Fraud Trends and Merchants' Response.* http://www.security.iia.net.au/downloads/2004_fraud_report.pdf (visited July 6, 2006).

5. http://www.securedecisions.com/documents/CostsOfBreaches-SANSInstitute.doc (visited July 6, 2006).

6. BBC News. 2001. Mafiaboy hacker jailed. September 13. http://news.bbc.co.uk/1/hi/sci/tech/1541252.stm (visited July 6, 2006).

7. http://www.usdoj.gov/criminal/cybercrime/melissaSent.htm (visited July 6, 2006).

6 | TRENDS IN CYBERCRIME

The term "digital divide" refers to the uptake and penetration of digital technology that has occurred unevenly around the world. Table 4-1 provides a snapshot of this distribution. What is new in a highly "wired" country may not yet appear on the radar screen of a country that has just entered the digital age.

This, of course, does have its blessings for some. Countries that are lagging in the uptake of digital technology can learn from the experiences of the digitally advantaged. But there is a downside. Countries that are "digitally challenged" may still lack the capacity to defend themselves against electronic criminal exploitation. What limited assets they have will be even more vulnerable. Although details are understandably sketchy, it was alleged some years ago that cybercriminals nearly succeeded in transferring the assets of the national bank of a small island nation into their own accounts elsewhere. And just as transnational organized criminals are able to use weak and failing states as "criminal havens," so, too, may digitally challenged countries serve as "*electronic* criminal havens."

SOPHISTICATION

Three basic trends in cybercrime have become apparent in the first decade of the new millennium. The first is *sophistication*. Cybercrime is becoming more sophisticated. Thompson (2004) described the highly creative virus writers who design malicious code of great complexity. Here are some general examples:

- The speed with which viruses infect computers around the world has increased dramatically in recent years. In 2001, the Code Red Virus infected 150,000 computer systems in fourteen hours; a mere two months later, the NIMDA virus spread across the United States in just one hour, attacking 86,000 computers (White House 2003).

- Hacking tools are becoming more powerful and easier to use. The term "intelligent malware" has been used to describe malicious code that seeks out vulnerable systems and/or covers its own tracks.

CRIMINAL EXPLOITATION OF WIRELESS TECHNOLOGY

The advent of wireless technology, for all its benefits, is creating new criminal opportunities. Wireless local area networks (LANs) are vulnerable to penetration. All one needs in order to access an internal wireless network is a computer, a wireless local area network card that costs less than $100, and software that is downloadable from the web. The term "war driving" has been coined to refer to the act of locating and logging wireless access points (or "hot spots") while in motion. Toward the end of 2003, one began to see prosecutions for unauthorized access to wireless systems from "mobile hackers." In November of that year, two men in Michigan were charged with cracking a home improvement store's nationwide network from a car parked outside one of the stores (U.S. Department of Justice 2004c).

- Webpages may be counterfeited in such a manner that the fake will be indistinguishable from the original legitimate page. The fake page may communicate false or misleading information in furtherance of an investment solicitation.
- Techniques of "phishing" have been refined in such a manner that apparently legitimate weblinks are placed in e-mail messages. When activated, the site will mimic a genuine webpage and invite the visitor to confirm his or her account number and PIN.

COMMERCIALIZATION

The second major trend is *commercialization*. If crime does follow opportunity, you can be sure that where there is money to be made, cybercriminals will try their hand. Today, more and more commercial activity occurs in an online environment. By definition, this creates an increasing number of opportunities for criminal exploitation. It follows that the incidence of cybercrime with a financial motive may be expected to increase.

Cyberspace illegalities that have not previously been characterized by commercialism are becoming increasingly subject to financial motivation. Consider child pornography. The earliest forms of Internet child pornography entailed noncommercial exchange or barter between collectors. Little, if any, commercial activity was evident (Grant, David, and Grabosky 2001). More recently, commercial exchange has become apparent, with service providers who are able and willing to refer users to illicit content sites for a fee (BBC News 2002). Today, entrepreneurial children equipped with webcams operate commercial sites using credit card payment processing companies to manage the revenue generated by their home-produced images and online sexual performances (Eichenwald 2005).

Similar patterns once characterized unauthorized access to computer systems and the dissemination of malicious code. At the dawn of the digital age, hackers and virus writers were amateurs (albeit sometimes very competent ones). Today, the term "hacker-for-hire" is becoming more familiar, and there are those virus writers who work on a fee-for-service basis.

The ability to communicate instantly with millions of people at little or no cost is not lost on legitimate marketers or on criminal fraudsters. If a message sent to a million recipients elicits responses from a mere one-tenth of 1 percent of them, this still adds up to one thousand prospective victims. The collection and sale of active e-mail addresses serves a niche market. There are entrepreneurs who harvest valid e-mail addresses for sale to legitimate commercial interests as well as to criminals. "Botnets" are rented out to spammers and phishers.

The numerous opportunities for criminal exploitation of cyberspace are quite apparent to criminal organizations. One may expect to see organized crime embrace digital technology with increasing enthusiasm in the years ahead.

INTEGRATION

The third important trend in cybercrime is *integration*. As is the case with terrestrial crimes, cybercrimes are not always committed in isolation. For example, armed robbers may steal a motor vehicle to travel to the scene of the robbery and to facilitate a getaway. So it is that certain types of cybercrime will entail a combination of different criminal acts. A recent development is the integration of distinct forms of computer crime to achieve synergies. Consider the following: Unsolicited electronic mail or "spam" may contain malicious code that can be activated if the recipient opens the mail or clicks on a link (such as one that reads "Click Here for Free Teen Sex Pix"). This code can be designed so that, if activated, it will allow the offender to "commandeer" the infected computer and use it in furtherance of criminal purposes. This can entail recording the victim's password and credit card details, or it may entail directing the victim's computer against another target. This latter scenario combines the scope of a virus infection with the intensity of a distributed denial-of-service attack. Such an attack may in turn be an element of extortion.

A number of additional trends in electronic crime are worth noting. These include the involvement of juveniles, the use of cryptography, and, as we will see in Chapter 7, the cross-border nature of much cybercrime.

THE INVOLVEMENT OF JUVENILES

The tremendous power that digital technology places in the hands of ordinary individuals extends to juveniles as well. Some of the more notorious cybercrimes have been committed by individuals of relatively tender years (DeMarco 2001). The criminal exploits of the Massachusetts teenager who disabled communications to the air traffic control tower at the Worcester Regional Airport and the distributed denial-of-service attacks by Mafiaboy were described above.

In March 2004, another Massachusetts teenager went on an electronic rampage. He sent an e-mail to a Florida school that read:

> your all going to perish and flourish . . . you will all die
> Tuesday, 12:00 p.m.
> we're going to have a "blast"
> hahahahahaha wonder where I'll be? youll all be destroyed. im
> sick of your [expletive deleted]
> school and piece of [expletive deleted] staff, your all gonna
> [expletive deleted] die you pieces of crap!!!!

DIE MOTHER [expletive deleted] IM GONA BLOW ALL
YOU UP
AND MYSELF
ALL YOU NAZI LOVING MEXICAN FAGGOT BITCHES
ARE DEAD

As a result of this threat, the school was closed for two days.

Five months later, the same juvenile obtained unauthorized access to the internal network of a major ISP. In January 2005, he gained access to the internal system of a large telephone service provider, obtained information about one of the provider's customers, and posted it on the Internet. He also set up a number of telephone accounts without having to pay for them. Shortly thereafter, he used a portable wireless device to access the Internet and arranged with accomplices to communicate a bomb threat to a school in Massachusetts, necessitating the school's evacuation.

In June 2005, he contacted another telephone service provider that had terminated an account that a friend had fraudulently activated. He threatened to initiate a denial-of-service attack against the provider unless he was granted access to the provider's system. The demand was not met, and within ten minutes, an attack was launched that succeeded in shutting down a good deal of the provider's web operations.

After pleading guilty in a U.S. federal court, the youth was sentenced to eleven months' detention in a juvenile facility, followed by two years of supervised release. During these periods of detention and supervised release, he was prohibited from possessing or using any computer, cell phone, or other equipment with which to access the Internet (U.S. Department of Justice 2005d).

The involvement of juveniles in deeds that, if they were possible at all ten years ago, were almost exclusively the work of adults, is an intriguing development. Pontell and Rosoff (2005) have used the term "white-collar delinquency" to refer to this departure from the historical norm. It further complicates the problems of white-collar crime theorists, who note that persons of less than relatively high social status are committing most white-collar crime. White-collar delinquency also complicates the lives of prosecutors. Federal prosecutors, who traditionally have had little occasion to charge juveniles, now find themselves having to seek terms of incarceration for young offenders in order to make it very clear that certain kinds of online activity are totally unacceptable.

CRYPTOGRAPHY

The sophistication of cybercrime is compounded by the widespread availability of cryptography. Once the monopoly of military organizations and intelligence services, technologies for concealing the content of electronic communications from all but the intended recipient are now widely available. Encryption is ideally suited to those offenders who wish to communicate in furtherance of criminal conspiracies or who wish to conceal information that might be used against them in court. Such information might include records of criminal transactions or illicit images. In addition to cryptography and steganography, technologies enable individuals to conceal their identities online or to impersonate other users. These technologies make it very difficult to identify suspects (Morris 2004). A number of nations are moving toward compulsory disclosure of cryptographic keys subject to judicial oversight. Jurisdictions with constitutional protection against self-incrimination may deem it an aggravating circumstance or even a separate offense to use cryptography in furtherance of a crime.

Authorities in the United States must go to such extraordinary lengths to obtain encryption keys because the Fifth Amendment protects individuals against self-incrimination. The right to remain silent applies to the disclosure of encryption keys no less than to other potentially incriminating information. To compensate for this constitutional impediment, U.S. legislators have introduced legislation that would make it an offense to use encryption to conceal incriminating communication relating to a crime that is being committed or attempted.

Those countries unconstrained by a bill of rights have devised a simpler solution to the challenge of encryption. They simply require individuals to disclose encryption keys or face criminal charges. In the United Kingdom, this can entail imprisonment for up to two years; in Australia, six months.[1] In Europe, Article 6 of the Rome Convention could be a barrier to such compulsory disclosure, although the European Commission on Human Rights has restricted the scope of the article to oral statements. Nevertheless, European procedures for compulsory decryption would have to be formulated precisely in order to withstand judicial scrutiny.

THE THREAT TO PRIVACY

Well over a century ago, long before the dawn of the digital age, the issue of individual privacy was the subject of a seminal article in the *Harvard Law Review* (Warren and Brandeis 1890). The junior author, Louis Brandeis, went on to become a famous justice of the U.S. Supreme Court. One of the article's concerns was the "unauthorized circulation of portraits of private persons" (p. 195). With uncanny prescience, they observed that "[i]nstantaneous photographs and newspaper enterprise have invaded the sacred precincts of private and domestic life; and numerous mechanical devices threaten to make good the prediction that 'what is whispered in the closet shall be proclaimed from the housetops' " (p. 195).

Threats to privacy in the digital age emanate from three main sources: individual cybercriminals, commercial organizations, and the government. We have already seen how some criminals will engage in electronic voyeurism. Others will seek to steal personal financial information such as credit card and bank account details. Still others will intrude on your privacy by flooding your e-mail inbox with offers too good to be true. But violation of your privacy is by no means the monopoly of criminals.

Among the greatest threats to one's digital privacy are those posed by legitimate commercial entities (Grabosky, Smith, and Dempsey 2001, chap. 10). Most people leave their footprints all over cyberspace. Information about the websites you visit, the products you buy, and various other data, such as your age and place of residence, are scattered throughout cyberspace. Data-matching technologies enable the compilation of electronic dossiers in considerable detail. These may be bought and sold for marketing purposes.

At times, sensitive personal information may be disclosed by mistake. Data on patients of health systems have been inadvertently made public. Mass e-mailings may accidentally include the addresses of all intended recipients. Some people may be quite pleased that Amazon.com knows what books they buy. Others may not. A story is told about a telephone company that offered special discounts to customers who regularly call individual numbers. Legend has it that on one occasion, a housewife received a standard telephone bill, with just such an offer enclosed. In this case, the specified number was unfamiliar to her. Curiosity drove her to ring the number, and she found that the subscriber was having an affair with her husband.

In addition to surveillance by criminals and by legitimate businesses, the state poses a threat to personal privacy. Surveillance of citizens, by agents of government or by electronic means, has long been a technique employed by totalitarian governments, symbolized by the expression "Big Brother Is Watching You" (Orwell 1951).

The same technologies of data matching that permit the compilation of electronic dossiers are available to governments no less than to commercial entities. A Total Information Awareness Program was developed by the Defense Advanced Research Projects Agency (DARPA) to create a grand centralized database ostensibly for the purpose of detecting terrorist activity. The name was subsequently changed to Terrorism Information Awareness Program (Electronic Privacy Information Center 2005). A report by the General Accounting Office identified almost 200 data-mining projects, either operational or in the planning stage, across the U.S. federal government (U.S. General Accounting Office 2004). The fact that much of this was designed to improve customer service may be of no consolation, as benign collections may have sinister applications: U.S. Census data were used to identify Japanese Americans for internment during World War II (Seltzer and Anderson 2001).

Despite the existence of the Fourth Amendment to the U.S. Constitution and the exacting provisions of Title 18 of the U.S. Code (which authorize the interception of telecommunications under some circumstances, subject to judicial authorization), a citizen enjoys only a modicum of privacy. The Internet is, of course, subject to surveillance. The FBI has deployed network collection technologies (previously referred to as "Carnivore") on numerous occasions. The name was changed to a less threatening DCS 1000 (U.S. Federal Bureau of Investigation 2003). The law allows the government easier access to stored data than to data in transit. Messages stored on the server of an ISP are accessible pursuant to a subpoena, rather than a warrant for interception. America Online responds to over three hundred criminal warrants *per day* (Liptak 2006).

On December 16, 2005, the *New York Times* published an article reporting that President Bush secretly authorized surveillance on U.S. citizens and residents without the warrants ordinarily required by law (Risen and Lichtblau 2005). The Bush administration contended that it had legal authority consistent with the President's as Commander in Chief. The issue has the potential to become a titanic struggle over the constitutionality of the President's actions.

In January 2006, the U.S. Department of Justice, in the course of preparing a justification for a controversial Internet pornography law, subpoenaed logs showing common search terms and a list of websites indexed by Google's search engines. The request sought a "random sample of 1 million URLs" and "the text of each search string entered onto Google's search engine over a 1-week period."[2] Although the request did not seek the identity of individual users, the potential for future violations of privacy was not lost on the general public.

ENDNOTES

1. Regulation of Investigatory Powers Act (2000), § 49–55; Crimes Act, § 3LA.
2. *Gonzalez v. Google, Inc.* U.S. District Court (N.D. Cal.). January 18, 2006: 3. http://www.mindfully.org/Reform/2006/Gonzales-v-Google18jan06.htm (visited June 9, 2006).

7 | INVESTIGATION, PROSECUTION, AND SENTENCING

INVESTIGATION

As is the case with terrestrial crime, cybercrime may come to the attention of the authorities while in progress or after the fact. In either case, it may not be apparent who the offender is or where he or she is physically situated.

The initial indicium of cybercrime is usually an attempt at unauthorized access. That is, someone is trying to get into a computer where he or she should not be. When such an intrusion is first detected, it may not be apparent whether the intruder is a teenage adventurer, a technician working for an organized criminal group, or the intelligence service of a foreign state.

The more inept cybercriminals will leave their tracks in numerous places. Their offending communications will be traceable to Internet Protocol (IP) addresses whose physical locations will be obvious. The more sophisticated offenders, who impersonate other users, who "loop" and "weave" their communications across a number of jurisdictions, and who conceal the content of their communications by encrypting them, pose the more difficult challenge.

Electronic crime scenes can vary substantially as well. Crimes can be initiated from a workstation within a large organization or from the comfort of an offender's bedroom. The targets of electronic crime may be widely dispersed, as is the case with computer viruses, or very localized, as is the case with computer stalking. Evidence may be found at the physical location of the perpetrator or the victim or at numerous locations throughout cyberspace.

The nature of the investigation will depend on the preferences of the victim and the priorities of the investigator. These may not always coincide. As we have noted, many institutional victims, such as banks, may not wish the world to know that their systems have been successfully attacked. Their main concerns are securing their systems (i.e., hardening the target) and recovering their losses, if possible. If the offender is an insider or a disgruntled former employee, this can, in some cases, be achieved without resort to prosecution. A veritable industry of private forensic computing specialists (many of whom are former police officers with expertise in computer crime investigation) exists for this purpose. If the organization is dependent on information technology for most of its business (especially the case with e-commerce), it is important that the system remain up and running as close to normal as possible.

Police, on the other hand, are primarily concerned with gathering evidence sufficient to obtain a conviction in a court of law. One can envisage circumstances in which the private interests of the victim conflict with what the police regard as the public interest. In situations such as these, who should prevail?

Digital evidence of a crime may be commingled with a great deal of other information that is totally irrelevant to the investigation; the metaphor of the needle in the haystack is not entirely inappropriate. Even with automated search tools, finding that needle may be extremely difficult and time-consuming.

In circumstances where the system itself was the instrument of the offense, seizure of the entire system may be an option. But such a course of action may cause undue inconvenience and considerable loss to innocent proprietors and their clients. In one case, *Steve Jackson Games, Inc. v. United States Secret Service*, 36 F.3d 457 (5th Cir. 1994), the U.S. government seized hardware and data files from a small Texas games manufacturer and ISP. The disruption was severe, nearly putting the company out of business. The material seized was thought to contain evidence of an offense by one of the company's customers. Neither the company nor its owner was ever prosecuted. Eventually, a federal court awarded damages to the company.

Nowadays, as we live in an increasingly networked environment, seizure of an entire system is not only unrealistic, but also logistically impossible. A more appropriate option, where feasible, is to make two copies of the contents of a hard drive. One can then be used for analysis and the other sealed and kept as a backup. Making only one copy enhances the risk of loss or damage. It is important to preserve the integrity of evidence, lest the accused challenge it in court.

Search and Seizure

The American Revolution was fought, in part, because of the repressive practices of British colonial rule. It is not surprising that the Constitution of the new United States guaranteed certain protections against governmental heavy-handedness. In the words of the Fourth Amendment:

> The right of the people to be secure in their persons, houses, papers, and effects, against unreasonable searches and seizures, shall not be violated, and no Warrants shall issue, but upon probable cause, supported by Oath or affirmation, and particularly describing the place to be searched, and the persons or things to be seized.

MANAGING ENCRYPTED EVIDENCE

Investigators went to exceptional lengths to obtain an encryption key during the investigation of a member of a prominent organized crime family on the East Coast of the United States. The individual was under investigation for illegal gambling and loan sharking. A clandestine search of the subject's office revealed a computer, but investigators were unable to access an encrypted file that they suspected contained evidence of criminal activity.

The FBI obtained additional warrants, authorizing them to undertake another surreptitious entry and to install a device developed by FBI engineers known as a key logger system (KLS) on the subject's computer. This would record the password to the encrypted information. The device worked as intended, and the investigators successfully obtained access to the subject's encrypted file. Based on the evidence contained in the file, the government charged him with a number of offenses.

The defense was unsuccessful in challenging the validity of the warrants, and the accused pleaded guilty in February 2002 (Electronic Privacy Information Center 2003).

Nowadays, technologies of remote search are making devices such as the KLS largely obsolete.

Much, much later, as technologies enabled the interception of communications between private citizens, protections against wiretapping and other forms of electronic eavesdropping were also introduced. Because of the particularly intrusive nature of telecommunications interception, requirements for a warrant are particularly stringent (U.S. Department of Justice 2002b). Investigators ignore these constraints at their peril, for failure to comply with the law can result in an offender going free; in extreme cases, it can result in criminal charges being laid against the investigator.

In some cases, evidence may be obtainable in publicly accessible locations. To this end, law enforcement agencies have designed elaborate ruses to trap computer criminals. In a 1995 operation codenamed "Operation Cybersnare," the U.S. Secret Service covertly established an Internet discussion group that served as a forum for the purchase of stolen cellular phone access numbers, credit card numbers, and personal identity information. Criminals joining the group who offered illicit products for sale were identified and prosecuted.[1]

For over a decade, law enforcement officers have posed online as children in order to trap adults in search of illicit assignations, and the practice is common in many Western democracies (Smith, Grabosky, and Urbas 2004, 190; Krone 2005b). Other countries do not permit online investigations, regarding them as an excessive use of police power. Undercover patrolling of the Internet can encroach on personal privacy and can inhibit freedom of expression, not only of criminals, but also of innocent persons.

Collecting, Preserving, Analyzing, and Presenting Digital Evidence

One of the most significant differences between cybercrime and terrestrial crime is the nature of the evidence. There are differences in the form it takes, the means by which it is stored, the place where it is located, the way in which it is found, and the physical limitations of what it will tell you. Digital evidence is intangible. It is often volatile. And it may also be massive in quantity, thereby posing substantial logistical challenges.

Nevertheless, the basic principles remain the same for handling digital evidence as for handling physical evidence (McKemmish 1999). Ideally, examination of the evidence does not entail alteration or modification of the data. The original data is preserved and copied, and any examination is carried out on the copy. Any changes to the original, if necessary, should be explicitly documented and justified, in order to minimize defense challenges to its integrity. In court, the evidence should be presented in a manner that does not change its meaning.

There are three basic issues arising from the use of electronic evidence. First, as discussed above, the defense may question the identity of the author of the evidence in question ("It wasn't me; it was somebody else."). Second, the defense can claim that the evidence was tampered with. Third, the defense can argue that the unreliability of computer programs created inaccuracies in the output.

Efforts to standardize forensic procedures have occurred on a number of fronts. The Computer Crime and Intellectual Property Section of the U.S. Department of Justice developed Federal Guidelines for Searching and Seizing Computers in 1994. The guidelines have been revised and updated periodically since then, most recently in 2002 (U.S. Department of Justice 2002b).

In March 1998, the International Organization on Computer Evidence (IOCE) was established to develop international principles for the procedures relating to digital evidence, to ensure the harmonization of methods and practices among nations, and to guarantee the ability to use digital evidence collected by one nation in the courts of another nation.[2]

Standardized forensic procedures have also been developed by the FBI's Computer Analysis Response Team (CART). In the United States, courts have given their imprimatur to certain standardized forensic practices. A recent example of best practices in search and seizure of computer evidence is provided in *United States v. Triumph Capital Group* (211 F.R.D. 31 (D. Conn. 2002)). There the defense in a public corruption case moved to suppress evidence that was seized from a laptop computer. The judgment described in great detail the steps taken at each stage of the search; it was, and remains, a textbook lesson in computer forensics. In the United Kingdom, the Association of Chief

Police Officers has drafted guidelines in relation to preferred forensic procedures.[3]

This developing standardization of forensic practices (assuming that investigators adhere to these standards) will give the defense less opportunity to challenge investigative techniques. Prosecutors should be aware that departures from recognized best practices, to the extent that they occur, are likely to be seized upon by defense counsel. In addition, the laws of evidence in a given jurisdiction should be able to accommodate the transformation of intangible evidence into a form intelligible to judges and juries.

One of the most important policy decisions relating to digital evidence concerns the extent to which telecommunications carriers and service providers may be required to assist law enforcement. In most developed nations, telecommunications infrastructure is privately owned, but subject to government regulation and license. The industry has a financial interest in retaining some information, such as transaction information (who contacted whom, when, and for how long) for billing purposes. But indefinite retention of digital information requires storage space, and storage costs money.

Precisely what financial burdens private industry should be required to bear in order to assist law enforcement is an important policy question. There is no simple answer, for the imposition of significant costs on industry may detract from profitability, which may in turn inhibit the growth of information technology and the economic development on which it will depend. In June 2006, it was reported that the U.S. Department of Justice, invoking the twin specters of terrorism and child pornography, suggested that it was considering policies that would require data retention for up to two years by ISPs.[4] Proposals for one-year retention requirements were already circulating in Congress (McCullagh 2006a, b).

The Global Context of Cybercrime Investigation

The challenge of investigating (and prosecuting) cybercrime when it occurs in one's own jurisdiction is daunting enough. When a cybercrime originates on the other side of the world, the problems are compounded.

First is the challenge of finding out where the offense originates. In order to conceal their location, cybercriminals physically present in one jurisdiction may "loop" or "weave" their attacks through a number of jurisdictions on the way to their target. Even in the absence of deliberate intent to conceal one's location, the nature of Internet traffic is such that criminal communications may cross jurisdictional boundaries as a matter of course. In one case involving the stalking of a woman in Hong Kong, investigators traced the offensive communication to a server in Colorado. Inquiries in Colorado revealed that the communication had originated in Hong Kong.

As we have seen, the identity of the offender and the nature of the offense may not be immediately apparent. An attempted intrusion may be the first step in a chain of successive crimes, and it may be the work of a teenage hacker, an organized crime group, or agents of a foreign government. Once it is determined that a computer crime has originated from a foreign jurisdiction, one must seek the cooperation of authorities in that jurisdiction to identify the suspect. This may be easier said than done, since authorities in other countries may lack the capacity to assist. They may simply not have officers with sufficient training in computer forensics to be of much help. They may also lack interest. Their priorities may simply lie elsewhere.

The fact that an offense (or elements of an offense) occurred on foreign soil raises complex questions, since issues of national sovereignty are at stake. For example, police officials from the People's Republic of China may not simply get on an airplane, fly to the United States, and execute a search on a computer located at the residence of a Falun Gong supporter in Los Angeles. Of course, technologies exist now where searches may be executed remotely, using many of the same methods that hackers do.

One of the murky areas of the law of cybercriminal procedure relates to the legal authority that is required in order to conduct such searches across national frontiers. Traditionally, obtaining cooperation from a foreign law enforcement agency required a formal and laborious process. Substantial documentation took time to prepare, and delays could arise in obtaining official signatures. Today, the speed with which cybercrime can be committed from one side of the world against a target on the other makes speedy cooperation in real time highly desirable. To this end, a group of technologically advanced nations have developed a 24/7 network of contacts to provide a platform for mutual assistance in transnational cybercrime cases.

Despite the challenges posed by the transnational nature of much cybercrime, there have been some stunning examples of success in the investigation and prosecution of offenses committed by participants in cross-national criminal conspiracies. Coordination is crucial to the interdiction of many criminal conspiracies because a raid on one conspirator alone can indicate to other participants that law enforcement may be on their trail and may inspire them to destroy incriminating evidence. The following are but a few examples of successful coordinated investigations.

Operation Cathedral. In the mid-1990s, a California woman's complaint that her daughter had been molested by the father of one of the girl's friends led to an international child pornography ring that convened in an Internet chat room. In the course of the investigation, an encryption key was discovered that led to an even larger ring, whose members used sophisticated encryption technology and who rotated the location of the host server in order to avoid detection. The investigation led to arrests of members in twelve different countries.

Operation Buccaneer. After a fourteen-month undercover operation, sixty-five searches were conducted in the United States and six foreign countries on December 11, 2001, against participants in an Internet copyright piracy conspiracy. Three British defendants were sentenced to terms of imprisonment of eighteen, twenty-four, and thirty months, respectively. The U.S. courts were more severe, imposing prison terms of thirty-three, forty-one, and forty-six months. The U.S. government sought extradition of an alleged conspirator resident in Australia, who, for obvious reasons, tenaciously challenged the application up to and including an unsuccessful application to the High Court of Australia (U.S. Department of Justice 2005e; *Griffiths v. United States of America & Anor*, [2005] HCATrans 666 (September 2, 2005)).

Operation Artus. At the end of 2001, German police executed a search warrant on a citizen suspected of offenses related to child pornography. It became apparent that the suspect had been exchanging incriminating material over an Internet relay chat (IRC) channel. He subsequently provided police with the nicknames of some of his correspondents. The investigation led to the execution of seven search warrants in the United States and thirty simultaneous searches in ten foreign countries.

Operation Falcon. This operation identified a company that provided credit card support services to sites in Belarus (a former republic of the USSR) that offered online child pornography on a commercial basis. The company, Regpay, Inc., allegedly processed nearly $3 million in subscription fees (Ashcroft 2004). By accessing transaction details of the company's customers, in cooperation with French, Spanish, and Belarusian authorities, U.S. investigators were able to identify suspected consumers of child pornography around the world. These leads were shared with law enforcement agencies in these suspects' home nations.

No fewer than 1,700 of these credit card transactions were referred to the Australian High Tech Crime Centre (AHTCC), leading to the identification in that country alone of over 700 potential suspects and the execution of more than 450 search warrants. According to the Commissioner of the Australian Federal Police, charges were brought against over 200 Australians (Keelty 2004).

PROSECUTION

Challenges faced by prosecutors in confronting cybercrime are in many respects similar to those faced in dealing with conventional crime. To the extent that they become involved in the planning and conduct of investigations (as is often the case in the United States), prosecutors must ensure that the investigative practices employed are consistent with applicable constitutional safeguards.

When presented with a case, prosecutors must decide whether the evidence is sufficient to sustain a conviction. Most prosecutors have more business than they can handle, and they must manage their resources to get the "biggest bang for the buck." In the United States, where the heads of most local prosecutors' offices are elected officials, career considerations, such as re-election as District Attorney or election to higher political office, may also be important. As such, prosecutors may be inclined to pursue high-profile murder cases rather than complex frauds or arcane high-tech crimes.

In the English-speaking world at least, most computer crime cases are disposed of by guilty plea. This is usually because prosecutors pursue matters where the evidence against the accused is overwhelming and the prospects of acquittal by a jury are remote. In such cases, the prospect of a lesser sentence following a plea of guilty is sufficient to persuade the defense to take that option.

Defenses

In some cases, an accused will take his or her chances with a jury. In 1993, a student at the University of Edinburgh was charged with unauthorized access to computer systems. This he did not dispute. His defense was based on the claim that he was addicted to computers. Obsession with computers is by no means unheard of; the Center for Online and Internet Addiction was founded in 1995.[5] In this case, the judge instructed the jury that mere addiction did not negate intent, but the jury voted to acquit. Despite this initial success, defenses based on addiction are not often used. After all, drug addiction is no defense to a charge of burglary. Rather, the defense will raise the matter of diminished capacity resulting from addiction in seeking a reduced sentence.

When a defendant facing very serious charges is confronted with a strong prosecution case and the prospects of a long prison term if convicted, he may be more inclined to go for broke. Such was the choice of an eighth-grade math teacher in Albany, Georgia, who set up a website advertising photos of young girls. A police search of his computer revealed an abundance of incriminating evidence, and the defense made a desperate case. Counsel contended that the accused was a vigilante who was working undercover to expose Internet predators and child pornographers. It was further argued that his computer was hacked by a Trojan horse virus. His defense failed, and he was sentenced to 17½ years in prison (U.S. Attorney's Office, Middle District of Georgia 2005).

The Trojan horse defense has met with greater success in the United Kingdom (Brenner, Carrier, and Henninger 2004). One teenager from Shaftesbury, Dorset, was acquitted of charges arising from an alleged distributed denial-of-service attack that froze computers serving the Port of Houston, Texas. Although a forensic examination of the defendant's computer revealed hacker tools and no evidence of a Trojan infection, the jury acquitted. Another UK case never got to court when the accused, charged with possessing child pornography, was actually found to have had a Trojan program on his computer. Prosecutors concluded that they had insufficient evidence to establish guilt beyond reasonable doubt and dismissed the charges.

The Trojan horse defense is not an insurmountable challenge for prosecutors, as the successful prosecution of the Georgia math teacher has shown. What is required for this, as for many ordinary cases, is complementary evidence consistent with guilt, ideally from a number of independent sources. The defendant's own level of computer literacy is one important factor. A person who is knowledgeable about computers and computer security should be less vulnerable to a Trojan infection than a naïve user. The existence of firewalls and current antivirus software on a suspect's computer makes a Trojan defense less credible.

Additional weight could be provided by evidence of the defendant's knowledge and intent. In child pornography cases, this could include a very large collection of images, stored in a variety of formats; a history of visiting chat rooms where such images are traded; other indicia of an interest in such material; or communication with known pedophiles. Finally, thorough forensic analysis of the suspect's computer is also essential, including definitive steps to determine the presence or absence of "malware" and, if found, to identify its capabilities. As jurors become more familiar with digital technology, it is likely that the mystique of the Trojan defense will dissipate, and it will become a decreasingly successful defense tactic. Meanwhile, careful forensic procedures will hasten this demise.

Another defense that has been used in extreme cases is the so-called fantasy defense, most common in prosecutions arising from alleged attempts to lure children for illicit purposes. Typically, the defendant will claim that his or her actions were an expression of fantasy and not indicative of real intentions. One defendant was charged in 1999 with traveling from Seattle to Santa Monica for the purpose of meeting a person who had identified herself as a thirteen-year-old girl (the "girl" turned out to be an FBI agent). The defendant argued that almost everyone in chat rooms engages in what he called "real-time" fiction, or role playing, and that the person he would meet in Santa Monica could just as easily have been a forty-year-old woman. His travel to Santa Monica therefore was not for the purpose of committing a crime. After four days of deliberation, the jury was unable to reach a verdict. All but one of the men on the jury accepted the fantasy defense, while the six women did not. Pessimistic about the prospects of a fantasy defense in a retrial, the defendant pleaded guilty to interstate travel with intent to engage in criminal sexual activity and received a relatively lenient sentence of nine months' in-home detention, five years' probation, and a fine of $20,000 (Smith, Grabosky, and Urbas 2004, 190).

Exemplary Prosecutions

Among the strategies used by governments to respond to cybercrime have been exemplary prosecutions, often coupled with stern warnings not to follow in the footsteps of the targeted offender. Such firm utterances are characteristic of prosecutors generally, but in the early years of cybercrime, they have been particularly noticeable. Their purpose is to counteract the ambivalence with which many people view certain types of cybercrime, especially hacking and piracy.

Following the arrest of an Israeli hacker charged with a series of intrusions into U.S. military information systems, U.S. Attorney

General Janet Reno said, "This arrest should send a message to would-be computer hackers all over the world that the United States will treat computer intrusions as serious crimes. We will work around the world and in the depths of cyberspace to investigate and prosecute those who attack computer networks" (U.S. Department of Justice 1998). Words such as "We will find them and bring them to justice" are common public utterances of prosecutors.

SENTENCING

Determining an appropriate penalty to impose on a convicted cyber-criminal is easier said than done. The aims of punishment are numerous, sometimes contradictory, and hardly embraced by everyone. They include

- Deterrence (both of the convicted offender and of those who might be tempted to follow in his or her footsteps),
- Rehabilitation of the offender,
- Denunciation of the crime in question,
- Retribution (exacting vengeance against the offender),
- Incapacitation of the offender,
- Restitution or compensation to the victim of crime, and
- Reconciliation and reintegration of the offender.

In addition to choosing a punishment that meets one or more of these objectives, a sentencing authority usually seeks to ensure that the penalty is *proportionate*—that it reflects the circumstances of the crime and that it is *appropriate to the background of the offender*. One could be forgiven for suggesting that this is often a "mission impossible."

Those cybercriminals who are unfortunate enough to get convicted in a court of law will receive a sentence of some kind. The nature and severity of that sentence will vary from one jurisdiction to another, depending on the perceived heinousness of the offense and the background of the offender. There have been no large-scale systematic analyses of cybercrime sentencing. A small study conducted by Smith, Grabosky, and Urbas (2004) found that cybercrime sentences appear to be no more or less severe than those imposed on similarly situated terrestrial offenders.

The two types of cybercrime that result in the stiffest sentences in the United States are offenses relating to child pornography and offenses relating to theft or piracy of intellectual property. In the United States, the most egregious cases of Internet child pornography result in sentences of just under twenty years' imprisonment; the more serious software piracy cases result in prison sentences of approximately five years.

In the United States, apparent disparities in sentences imposed by federal judges led to the creation of the U.S. Sentencing Commission in 1984. At issue was the principle that similar crimes, committed by similar offenders, should receive similar punishments. Within the statutory maximum and minimum sentences prescribed by Congress for each federal offense, the Sentencing Commission developed a set of guidelines to inform judicial discretion. Upward and downward departures within these guidelines could occur, depending on the presence or absence of aggravating or mitigating circumstances, respectively.

The sentencing guidelines have always been controversial. Federal judges, in particular, were concerned that their sentencing discretion was severely limited. The status of the guidelines has changed in light of subsequent litigation. In *United States v. Booker*, 543 U.S. 220 (2005) the U.S. Supreme Court held that facts (such as the amount of drugs involved in a sale) that might serve as the basis for an increased sentence under the guidelines must be determined by a jury and that the guidelines could no longer be mandatory, but rather only advisory.

What is important for the sentencing of cybercriminals is what the guidelines refer to as a "special skills enhancement." That is, an offender who uses special skills (such as those of a pilot, accountant, or chemist) that significantly facilitate the commission or the concealment of an offense may receive an increased sentence as a result. In the early years of the digital age, the digital divide between "tech-savvy" computer jocks and computer illiterates raised the question, Just what constitutes the use of special skills in the commission of a cybercrime?

One offender had no formal computer training, but was sufficiently skilled to gain unauthorized access to the computers of Pacific Bell in order to facilitate intercepting and seizing the telephone lines of a radio station. Two of his accomplices had discovered a computer program that could be used to "rig" the results of the radio station's promotional contests to ensure that they were the correct caller to win various prizes. Using this information, the offender called the radio station and "won" a $10,000 cash prize. The accomplices "won" at least two Porsche automobiles, a $20,000 cash prize, a $10,000 cash prize, and two trips to Hawaii. In addition, the offender was able to break into other sophisticated computer systems, place wire taps on phones, and transfer large sums of money between banks. Although the sentencing guidelines provided that special skills "usually" require substantial education, training, or licensing, the offender received a special skills enhancement for his efforts because the skills in question were of a high level and not possessed by members of the general public (*United States v. Petersen*, 98 F.3d 502 (9th Cir. 1996)).

In another illustration of the use of special skills in furtherance of cybercrime, the accused hacked into a company's computer network and illegally installed a secure shell account that gave him continuing remote access. He used the system to store hacking programs and other information and also installed a "sniffer" program to intercept and record communications on the network. Using this information, he obtained access to a second company's network and deleted the company's entire database. For good measure, he left a message that said, "Hello, I have just hacked into your system. Have a nice day." The defendant's computer expertise in furtherance of these crimes earned him a special skills enhancement, adding up to a twenty-seven-month prison term (U.S. Department of Justice 2001b).

But the special skills enhancement does have its limits in the digital age. In one case, the defendant, who had no formal training in computing, bought Adobe Page Maker®, an off-the-shelf software package. He learned how to use the program with the assistance of a high school friend over the course of a week and began scanning and duplicating U.S. currency. The district court held that the defendant made use of special skills, but the appeals court found that the defendant's computer skills were not "particularly sophisticated" compared to those in *Petersen* and thus found that the enhancement was unwarranted (*United States v. Godman*, 223 F.3d 320 (6th Cir. 2000)).

A closer call was made in a case arising from website counterfeiting. The defendant registered the domain name "www.honolulu-marathon.com," which was very close to that of the official site of the Honolulu Marathon Association: "www.honolulu-marathon.org." He then created a website that was almost identical to the official site, but that also contained an online registration form in Japanese to receive registrants' credit card numbers (no such facility was available on the official site). The defendant was subsequently convicted of wire fraud in the U.S. district court, which found that he "was skilled at accessing and manipulating computer systems" and imposed the special skills enhancement. On appeal, the court held that the skills required to counterfeit a webpage were more like Godman's than Petersen's and not in the class of "pilots, lawyers, doctors, accountants, chemists, and demolition experts." The special skills enhancement was disallowed (*United States v. Lee*, 296 F.3d 792 (9th Cir. 2002)).

As digital technology becomes increasingly pervasive in everyday life, it thus appears that only those truly expert in computing will receive sentence enhancements for the application of their talents in furtherance of crime. Ordinary offenders will receive ordinary sentences.

Another consideration in sentencing cybercriminals relates to what restrictions, if any, should be placed on the offender as conditions of probation or parole. It is quite common, for example, to require that an offender refrain from consuming alcohol or drugs; convicted child sex offenders are often prohibited from associating with children. Computer criminals may be required to forfeit the equipment used in the commission of an offense; this is appropriate as long as the equipment in question is theirs, and not their employer's or someone else's. Somewhat more controversial are restrictions on the offender's access to and use of digital technology.

Perhaps the most prominent case to date is that of Kevin Mitnick, who was subject to a complete prohibition (without prior approval of his probation officer) on the possession or use of practically any kind of equipment that could be used to access a computer system or network. He was further prevented from serving as a consultant or advisor to anyone engaged in computer-related activity. Mitnick appealed this order on the grounds that it was overly excessive and infringed his First Amendment rights. The appeals court, however, held that the conditions were reasonable in light of the appellant's record of recidivism.

The ubiquity of digital technology may make restrictions as severe as those imposed on Mitnick a thing of the past. In a more recent case, the offender was prohibited from possessing or using a computer equipped with a modem allowing access to any part of the Internet. He appealed successfully, the judge observing that "such

POSTRELEASE RESTRICTIONS IMPOSED ON KEVIN MITNICK

Without the prior express written approval of the probation officer:

- The defendant shall not possess or use, for any purpose, the following:
- Any computer hardware equipment;
- Any computer software programs;
- Modems;
- Any computer-related peripheral or support equipment;
- Portable laptop computers, "personal information assistants," and derivatives;
- Cellular telephones;
- Televisions or other instruments of communication equipped with on-line, Internet, world-wide web, or other computer network access;
- Any other electronic equipment, presently available or new technology that becomes available, that can be converted to or has as its function the ability to act as a computer system or to access a computer system, computer network or telecommunications network (except defendant may possess a "land line" telephone);
- The defendant shall not be employed in or perform services for any entity engaged in the computer, computer software, or telecommunications business and shall not be in any capacity wherein he has access to computers or computer-related equipment or software;
- The defendant shall not access computers, computer networks, or other forms of wireless communications himself or through third parties;
- The defendant shall not act as a consultant or advisor to individuals or groups engaged in any computer-related activity;
- The defendant shall not acquire or possess any computer codes (including computer passwords), cellular phone access codes, or other access

> devices that enable the defendant to use, acquire, exchange, or alter information in a computer or telecommunications database system;
>
> - The defendant shall not use or possess any data encryption device, program or technique for computers;
>
> - The defendant shall not alter or possess any altered telephone, telephone equipment, or any other communications-related equipment;
>
> - The defendant shall only use his true name and not use any alias or other false identity. (Painter 2001, 2)

a ban renders modern life—in which, for example, the government strongly encourages taxpayers to file their returns electronically, more and more commerce is conducted online, and where vast amounts of government information are communicated via website—exceptionally difficult" (*United States v. Holm*, 326 F.3d 872 (7th Cir. 2003, 877–878)).

It therefore appears that restrictions imposed on cybercriminals will be less stringent. A more recent judgment indicates the kinds of strategies likely to be adopted in the future: "We are confident that the district court can impose a more narrowly-tailored restriction on Mr. Crume's computer use through a prohibition on accessing certain categories of websites and Internet content and can sufficiently ensure his compliance with this condition through some combination of random searches and software that filters objectionable material" (*United States v. Crume*, 422 F.3d 728, 733 (8th Cir. 2005)).

ENDNOTES

1. http://www.bbsdocumentary.com/library/CONTROVERSY/RAIDS/CYBERSNARE (visited June 8, 2006).

2. http://www.ioce.org (visited June 8, 2006).

3. http://www.acpo.police.uk/asp/policies/Data/gpg_computer_based_evidence_v3.pdf (visited June 8, 2006).

4. For a European perspective on data retention, see http://www.epic.org/privacy/intl/data_retention.html (visited June 13, 2006).

5. http://www.netaddiction.com/company_info.htm (visited June 8, 2006).

8 | CONCLUSION: THE FUTURE OF ELECTRONIC CRIME AND ITS CONTROL

Society will continue to benefit from all the advantages bestowed on us by digital technology. New applications, as yet unforeseen, will revolutionize the way we do things. But these developments will also provide new opportunities for criminals. Cybercrime will continue to challenge us. As more and more people from the less advantaged side of the digital divide cross over and enjoy more of the benefits of digital technology, they will contribute to the ranks of potential offenders and prospective victims. The arms race between those who seek to refine criminal applications of high technology and those who would interdict them will continue.

Cybercrime is sufficiently diverse and widespread that its effective prevention and control will require the efforts of many individuals and institutions. Just as police in Western industrial societies acknowledge that the effective reduction of terrestrial crime will require partnerships with industry and with the community, so it is with responses to cybercrime. Let us explore the most productive strategies to combat cybercrime from the perspective of routine activity theory.

STRATEGIES BASED ON ROUTINE ACTIVITY THEORY

Motivation

Prospects for reducing the supply of motivated offenders must be regarded as limited. As noted earlier, the motivations for many types of cybercrime are deeply engrained in the human behavioral repertoire. There is not a great deal that can be done to make people less greedy, less lustful, and less vengeful in cyberspace or on the ground. Moreover, the idea of "pulling the plug" and restricting access to digital technology is becoming increasingly unrealistic, even as a condition of parole for convicted offenders.

This is not to say that constructive work cannot be done at the margins to improve civility in cyberspace. Regardless of when people are introduced to digital technology, they are in a position to learn basic rules of ethics and etiquette. A culture of cyberspace civility can be learned. If informal socialization processes are insufficient to impress on people what kinds of behaviors are unacceptable, governments appear more than willing to step in. Among the functions of the criminal law is the reaffirmation of society's values, and (at least in the United States) the stiff penalties prescribed for acts such as denying service, disseminating child pornography, or pirating software make at least some would-be offenders think twice.

There was a time in America when racism was socially acceptable. Now it is not. At the dawn of the digital age, the hacker's ethic and the view that all information should be free were widely embraced and were not forcefully challenged (Levy 1984, 27). They are challenged now.

One imaginative suggestion for changing hacker culture is to sponsor hack-in contests, offering positive incentives for those who channel their energies in lawful ways (Wible 2003). The closest terrestrial equivalent would appear to be the urban art movement that seeks to transform graffitists into muralists. Such a program might divert a few individuals from engaging in illegal hacking, but its potential effects on the determinedly rebellious hacker or the hacker for hire are certainly questionable. Nor would strategies like this be generalizable to child pornographers or fraudsters.

Opportunity

The first line of defense against cybercrime is self-defense. Individuals and institutions with assets to protect are well advised to take basic security precautions commensurate with the risks they face. Individual users, for example, should safeguard their passwords and PINs. They should invest in basic security software such as virus scanners. Organizations such as financial institutions, major retailers, and governmental agencies that may be attractive targets are likely to invest more heavily in information technology security.

Market forces, too, will militate in favor of cybercrime control. While initial system architecture and software applications were once designed for convenience (often at the expense of security), today security is given a higher priority. Since system integrity depends almost entirely on software, products are being designed for greater robustness, with fewer accessible "backdoors."

Security and prosperity in cyberspace will depend significantly on market forces. Those financial institutions that provide secure platforms for online banking will flourish; those that do not will wither. Those companies that develop operating systems that optimize user-friendliness and security will earn billions. The software and entertainment industries are devoting considerable energies to the development of technologies that will make their products more difficult for information pirates to reproduce.

New technologies of access control such as biometric authentication have tremendous potential to contribute to the "hardening" of electronic targets. As the cost of these technologies decreases and as their accuracy improves, this will significantly reduce opportunities for unauthorized access to information systems.

Guardianship

One of the most important strategies for the prevention and control of cybercrime is to increase public awareness of the risks that private individuals and institutions face and how best to minimize them. This is important, given the finite capacity of the state to control what goes on in cyberspace. There may have been times and places when commerce

---

BIOMETRIC AUTHENTICATION

The United Kingdom Biometrics Working Group (2006) defines biometric authentication as "the automated means of recognising a living person through the measurement of distinguishing physiological or behavioural traits." Biometric techniques include the following:

Signature dynamics: Differences in pressure and writing speed at specific points in the signature.

Typing patterns: Time intervals between characters and overall speeds and patterns.

Fingerprint scanners: Unique features of fingerprints.

Hand or palm geometry: Lengths and angles of individual fingers.

Facial recognition: Location of the nose and eyes; configuration of the eye sockets, the areas around the cheekbones, and the sides of the mouth.

Voice recognition: Verification of speech patterns.

Eye scans: Distinguishing characteristics of the retina or iris.
(Kay 2005)

---

and critical infrastructure were state monopolies, but this is certainly not the case today.

It might be said that guardianship begins at home. Few parents are perfect, and protection of children from electronic harm will sooner or later clash with a young person's desire for privacy and personal space. Some very creative work has been done by nongovernmental organizations to confront the risks posed by information technology. Netsafe, an Internet safety group in New Zealand that has received international recognition, is one such example.[1] Netsafe provides basic information for parents, schools, small businesses, and other organizations on how to maintain basic computer security.

A significant component of capable guardianship is the prospective offender's perception that he or she is under surveillance. To be sure, there are certain steps that individuals can take to mask their identity, cover their tracks, or conceal the content of their communications. Those of us who engage in Internet banking are grateful that our account numbers and access codes are shielded from public view. We are usually grateful that banks place a limit on the number and amount of withdrawals that we are allowed to make in a given period. On more than one occasion, I have been slightly embarrassed, but essentially pleased, to be contacted by my bank and queried about unusual charges made with my credit card. The bank was reassured to learn that the charges were all made by me.

PLURALISTIC PREVENTION AND CONTROL OF CYBERCRIME

Few, if any, governments in the world today are able to single-handedly provide for the security and prosperity of their citizens. This is no less the case in cyberspace than on the ground. Governments depend on the cooperation of various institutions in civil society. It follows that securing cyberspace will also necessarily be a pluralistic endeavor.

Manufacturers, whether motivated by a spirit of good corporate citizenship, consumer demand, or the specter of products liability litigation, are designing software and hardware products that are less vulnerable to criminal exploitation. Entire industries have developed to deliver security solutions, from encryption to firewalls, to biometric authentication devices. In November 2003, Microsoft announced the launch of its Antivirus Reward Program for information leading to the arrest and conviction of writers of malicious code.

Joint investigations involving public and private institutions are becoming increasingly common. One investigation involving cooperation among German law enforcement agencies, the U.S. Secret Service and FBI, and Microsoft led to the arrest of an individual responsible for the Netsky and Sasser worms in May 2004.

In the United States, the Direct Marketing Association hired fifteen investigators to work with the FBI and other governmental agencies on antispam activity. The Australian High Tech Crime Centre in Canberra includes technicians from Australia's major financial institutions, whose salaries are paid by their banks and who work shoulder-to-shoulder with law enforcement officers.

Among those with a significant interest in controlling spam are ISPs, whose systems, figuratively speaking, groan under the weight of excessive e-mail. It was estimated in 2004, for example, that Microsoft's Hotmail service received 2 billion pieces of junk e-mail each day (Hansell 2004).

PRIVATE ENFORCEMENT

Corporate image is inherently valuable. When damaged, it can be very costly to repair. So it is that some companies engage private investigators to patrol cyberspace to ensure that their corporate websites have not been maliciously altered or counterfeited. Internet auction companies guard against use of their services to sell stolen goods or other contra-band (Rustad 2001). The motion picture, music, and software industries have developed considerable capacity to detect piracy, to assist govern-ments in investigation and prosecution, and to undertake private civil action against offenders.

Private civil remedies may also contribute to the control of cyber-crime. Just as street offenses such as drug dealing can be addressed by private civil remedies, such as suits for violation of nuisance laws (Mazerolle and Ransley 2006), so, too, can a variety of cybercrimes. Moreover, civil remedies require a significantly lower burden of proof—in common law countries, the balance of probability rather than beyond a reasonable doubt.

Numerous examples of the state creating specified rights, confer-ring them on private parties, and leaving it up to those private parties to enforce may be seen in the area of music and video piracy. Where the capacity and the priorities of public police preclude criminal investiga-tion of music, video, or software piracy, a victim of piracy may be able to seek civil remedies. In the United States, the Recording Industry Association of America (RIAA) has sued over 10,000 individuals for allegedly pirating music online.[2] In 2003, the Motion Picture Association achieved resolution of two civil actions in relation to DVD piracy in the Beijing Second Intermediate People's Court and six such actions in the People's Courts of Shanghai. The terms of the settlements included the following: ceasing further replication and destroying all copies, making formal apologies, paying penalties averaging $10,000 per case, and agreeing to pay increased penalties if unauthorized repli-cation recurs (Motion Picture Association 2003a, 2003b).

Engineering institutions have emerged and evolved in furtherance of cybercrime control. In the aftermath of the Morris worm in 1988, a Computer Emergency Response Team (CERT) was established at

Carnegie Mellon University in Pittsburgh, Pennsylvania, to coordinate responses to Internet security problems. CERT members are alerted to potential security threats against their systems and given advice on how best to avoid, minimize, and recover from damage (Carnegie-Mellon Software Engineering Institute 2005). In 2003, a national Computer Emergency Readiness Team (US–CERT) was established as part of the Department of Homeland Security.[3] Worldwide, there are more than 250 organizations with the acronym CERT that concern themselves with cybersecurity. It would appear that "coordinating the coordinators" will be a major challenge of the twenty-first century.

Negligent management of one's computer systems can lead to significant problems. Failure to supervise adequately an employee's use of the office computer system can lead to difficulties if, in the course of unauthorized surfing or e-mailing, the system contracts a virus or is penetrated by a Trojan horse. Harassment by one employee of another employee can land their employer in court. Because misuse of an organization's computer systems occurs from within its own ranks as well as at the hands of outsiders, a degree of internal guardianship is essential.

CYBERVIGILANTES

The appropriate role of private citizens in the control of cybercrime is a vexing issue. In cyberspace, as in the terrestrial world, it is usually not a good thing for a person to take the law into his or her own hands. The reasons for this should be self-evident. Consistency and fairness in the application of law are arguably best provided by the state.

The role of the private citizen in intelligence collection and law enforcement is not without precedent. Privateers and bounty hunters have a long, if not always glorious, tradition in the United States. The lynch mobs of the late nineteenth and early twentieth centuries were a particularly dark chapter in its history. Indeed, one of the virtues of the modern state (in theory at least) has been the development of exacting procedures for the administration of criminal justice within clearly defined structures of accountability.

Private citizens, even well-meaning ones, may not fully understand the consequences of their actions. For one, a hunt for pedophiles or terrorists in cyberspace may entail unauthorized access to or interference with a computer system, both of which are criminal offenses. For another, a private sleuth may inadvertently interrupt an ongoing investigation or may contaminate a crime scene. A "counter-hacker," striking back at the apparent source of an intrusion, may be unaware that his or her target, the proximate source of the offending communication, may be a mere tool commandeered by the true offender. It is not difficult to inflict a great deal of damage in cyberspace quite by accident.

The activities of private citizens vary in terms of intrusiveness. At one extreme are those who many encounter indicia of illegality in cyberspace and basically ignore it. Next, there are those who might call the matter to the attention of another private actor—perhaps a "cyber watchdog" or an Internet safety group such as the Cyber Angels.[4] Others may see fit to report it to an appropriate authority such as the U.S. Securities and Exchange Commission,[5] the Internet Crime Complaint Center,[6] or the CyberTipline of the National Center for Missing and Exploited Children.[7] Some will go further, perhaps entering a chat room pretending to be a fourteen-year-old, arranging for a meeting in physical space, and then showing up armed with a video camera. Images may then be posted on the web or details referred to police.[8]

Private citizens have been active in pursuing the perpetrators of advance-fee fraud schemes as well as child pornographers. Creating their own false identities, these "counter-scammers" seek to engage the real fraudsters. The most benign simply lead the fraudsters on by engaging them in endless correspondence or by (falsely) assuring them that a payment is available for collection at a Western Union office in a distant city. Some seek to collect financial and technical information to refer to law enforcement agencies. Others seek to embarrass or humiliate the fraudsters by getting them to pose for photographs. At the extreme, some seek to disable fraudulent bank websites or break into the fraudsters' e-mail accounts to identify and warn prospective victims (Schiesel 2004). For many, it is a kind of sport.[9]

An interesting issue, by no means close to definitive resolution, is the extent to which the government should compel third parties to assist in the prevention and control of cybercrime. For example, service providers are required to preserve records or other evidence in their possession when requested by the government, pending the issuance of a court order.[10] The South Carolina Criminal Code requires computer repair technicians who encounter evidence of child pornography to report this to law enforcement.[11]

In the United States, the Bill of Rights protects a citizen against an illegal search by the government, but not by a private citizen. In general, evidence obtained as the result of an illegal search by governmental agents will be inadmissible in court. Evidence obtained illegally by a private actor will be admissible in criminal proceedings as long as the government did not encourage or have prior knowledge of the illegal action. The following anecdote raises interesting questions about private third-party involvement in enforcing laws against cybercrime.

In July 2000, a police officer in Montgomery, Alabama, received an e-mail message and an attached image from "unknownuser1069@hotmail.com." The message read:

> I found a child molester on the net. I'm not sure if he is abusing his own child or a child he kidnapped. He is from Montgomery,

Alabama. As you see he is torturing the kid. She is 5–6 y.o. His face is seen clearly on some of the pictures. I know his name, Internet account, home address and I can see when he is online. What should I do? Can I send all the pics and info I have to these emails?

Regards

P.S. He is a doctor or a paramedic.

At the request of the police officer, "unknownuser," who later revealed that he was from Istanbul, Turkey, provided the IP address, name, street address, and fax number of a local Montgomery doctor. Based on this information, police obtained the appropriate warrants and arrested the suspect, who was tried, convicted, and sentenced to 17 1/2 years in prison. "unknownuser" was reluctant to identify himself to the police for one obvious reason: He had obtained access to the doctor's computer by illegal means. "unknownuser" had posted a file containing a version of the sub seven Trojan horse virus to the news group "alt.binaries.pictures.erotica.pre-teen." He claimed to have identified 2,000 other collectors of child pornography in that manner.

The doctor's appeal of his conviction was unsuccessful, the court holding *inter alia* that "unknownuser" had engaged in illegal activities without the knowledge or encouragement of the government and that the evidence obtained as a result was admissible (*United States v. Steiger*, 318 F.3d 1039 (11th Cir. 2003)).

But what about circumstances such as those anticipated by mandatory reporting legislation, where computer repair technicians are required to report apparent child pornography to police? Could it not be said that such legislation not only requires, but also *encourages* notification? The action required by the South Carolina Criminal Code is *notification*, not search (*United States v. Peterson*, 294 F.Supp. 2d 797 (D.S.C. 2003). One might also note that a person would have a lesser expectation of privacy in handing his computer over to a repair facility than in using it in the security of his home.

LEGISLATION

The substantive criminal law—the law that defines certain activities as criminal and prescribes punishment for those convicted of having committed them—must cover the range of harmful activities in which people can engage. In many cases, the elasticity of the existing criminal law will be adequate to cover many cybercrimes, and certainly the old crimes committed with new technologies. In some places, new legislation may be required, as was the case in the Philippines when it enacted a legislative "patch" in the aftermath of the ILOVEYOU virus.

The criminal procedure law—the law that governs the search for and seizure of evidence—must also be adapted to cyberspace. Techniques of investigation that were once the stuff of science fiction are now in common use. It is important that their use, and those who use them, be accountable and subject to the rule of law.

Finally, governments will continue to play a major role in securing cyberspace. Governmental responses to cybercrime require an adequate set of laws. Adequate substantive criminal legislation should be in place to prohibit current and emerging manifestations of cybercrime, and the laws of evidence and procedure should facilitate investigation and prosecution.

There are a number of issues that governments must consider in developing a legislative framework for the prevention and control of cybercrime. First is the substantive criminal law. It is important to spell out exactly which kind of conduct is criminal and which is not. The rule of law requires the avoidance of vagueness and ambiguity. The ordinary citizen should know what behavior is permitted and what is forbidden. In those countries that adhere most closely to the rule of law, uncertainties in criminal statutes are to be resolved in favor of the defendant.

Technology tends to develop faster than the law, so what one sees is a kind of catch-up. In some cases, very harmful conduct is simply not covered by the law. The person who released the ILOVEYOU virus in the Philippines escaped prosecution because the law of the Philippines did not make it a crime to release malicious code. In other cases, criminal prohibitions may not be specific, but the law will be sufficiently flexible to prohibit the harmful behavior in question.

A statute that criminalizes fraud, but only when perpetrated against human actors, may be challenged on the grounds that it does not extend to the deception of machinery. This would make it necessary to criminalize explicitly ATM-related fraud (*Kennison v. Daire*, 160 C.L.R. 129 (1986)). Certainly, a preference for technology-neutral language would be in order, given the risk that the law could become obsolete as a result of technological developments.

Nations on the privileged side of the digital divide tend to have adequate legislation in place. The most widely embraced model is the Council of Europe Cybercrime Convention, to date the most widespread and comprehensive initiative to bring international cooperation to cybercrime control. The convention seeks to achieve a degree of consistency in substantive criminal, evidence, and procedural laws, as well as expedited mutual assistance in cases of cybercrime committed across national frontiers. Even during its long drafting stage (lasting over four years and producing twenty-seven drafts), it provided guidance for non-European states involved in developing their own legislation. The Council of Europe formally adopted the Convention on Cybercrime in Budapest in November 2001. The convention came into force in July 2004.[12]

Legislative initiatives to control spam have been introduced in a number of countries; in the United States, the CAN SPAM Act became law in 2003. The next few years will provide an opportunity to see how it plays out in the courts. Among the more popular features are the requirement that the e-mail in question

- Contain clear and conspicuous identification as an advertisement,
- Include "opt-out" instructions permitting the recipient to exclude future unsolicited communications from the same source, and
- Include an "unsubscribe" facility.

Legislation may also make it an offense to use a false or misleading header or deceptive subject line. Some jurisdictions are considering prohibitions on the use of electronic address harvesting tools and of harvested address lists, predicates to the dissemination of spam. Between February 2005 and March 2006, three defendants pleaded guilty to aiding and abetting others to violate the CAN SPAM Act. The spam in question consisted of advertisements for pornographic websites, giving rise to more than 600,000 complaints to America Online.[13] The transmission of spam may also invite fraud-related charges, as was the case with the Phillies fan noted in Chapter 3.

In addition to the criminal sanction, it may be possible to use other remedies. Civil laws may allow suits for trespass to chattel; thus, purveyors of spam may be liable for interfering with the lawful use of a computer system if the system's disks are damaged or if one's lawful use is impeded by spam (Sorkin 2001; Magee 2003). Microsoft and a number of other prominent ISPs have used the civil justice system against spammers.

There may be no perfect solution for the problem of spam. Purveyors of "V1agra" can defeat blocking and filtering technologies. Some of these technologies can be too restrictive, screening out communications that one might actually want to see. It is difficult for legislative drafters to differentiate spam from other commercial communications and even from political communications, which are usually subject to a degree of protection in democratic societies. The risk of overregulation, with the adverse unintended consequences that so often accompany legislative intervention, cannot be overlooked. And as more and more commerce occurs in the online environment, it is important not to discourage legitimate commercial activity.

INTERNATIONAL COOPERATION

International cooperation in the prevention and control of cybercrime has intensified with the global increase in connectivity. Understandably, initiatives began in the industrialized world, where the risks of cybercrime were most apparent. In December 1997, the eight major industrialized nations (the G8) drew up a ten-point plan to confront transnational cybercrime. The major pillars were the development of a solid legislative base and the development of capacity among criminal justice professionals to deal with these crimes. As noted above, the Council of Europe Convention on Cybercrime seeks to achieve a degree of consistency in substantive criminal, evidence, and procedural laws, as well as expedited mutual assistance in cases of cybercrime committed across national frontiers.

THE FUTURE OF ELECTRONIC CRIME

Cybercrime is a moveable feast. It is tempting, but risky, to try to anticipate what the future holds in store for us. In 1990, I was asked by the Australian government to estimate the kinds of problems that they would be likely to encounter in the year 2000. I suggested that "junk faxes" might become a problem. The problems of spam and denial-of-service

FOREIGN PROSECUTION

A cybercrime committed from country A to country B, assuming a suspect has been identified and the behavior in question has violated the laws of both countries, raises the question of who will prosecute. Perhaps the easiest solution is to leave the matter to authorities in the country from which the perpetrator undertook the alleged criminal activity. It is a much less costly and time-consuming path to take than extradition. One example of the host country prosecuting a transnational offender is the case of a resident in Melbourne, Australia, who sent over three million e-mail messages to addressees in Australia and the United States with the intent of manipulating the price of shares of a company traded on the NASDAQ exchange in New York. He timed his own trades in the company's shares appropriately and pocketed a profit of around $15,000. In cases of this nature, it is common for the U.S. Securities and Exchange Commission to seek disgorgement of the ill-gotten gains and an injunction against the perpetrator to prevent reoffending. Rather than mobilizing the federal criminal process and seeking to extradite the offender, U.S. authorities were happy to leave prosecution to Australia. The accused pleaded guilty, was sentenced to prison for three years, and was released on probation after three months, subject to good behavior.[14]

attacks were nowhere on my radar screen. What we can say with certainty is that every new technology or device will have criminal applications.

We may be confident of one thing: Technology will not stand still. New technologies and applications, unforeseeable today, will be introduced in our lifetime. These technologies will expand our capacities and make life more exciting and fulfilling for many. Alas, they will also provide new opportunities for criminals. In the words of Rosoff, Pontell, and Tillman's First Law of Electronic Crime, *"If it can be done, someone will do it"* (Rosoff, Pontell, and Tillman, 1998, 366). A century ago the famous philosopher Santayana observed that those who forget the past are condemned to repeat it. Today, those who ignore the future are in for a rude shock when it arrives.

ENDNOTES

1. http://www.netsafe.org.nz (visited June 8, 2006).

2. Recording Industry Association of America. 2005. RIAA expands scope of illegal file-sharing lawsuits against student abusers of Internet. http://www.riaa.com/news/newsletter/052605.asp (visited June 9, 2006); RIAA Watch. 2005. 740 more sued: 10,777 total. May 27, 2005. http://www.riaa.com/news/newsletter/052605.asp (visited June 9, 2006).

3. http://www.us-cert.gov (visited June 8, 2006).

4. http://www.cyberangels.org (visited June 8, 2006).

5. enforcement@sec.gov.

6. http://www.ic3.gov (visited June 8, 2006).

7. http://www.cybertipline.com (visited June 8, 2006).

8. http://www.perverted-justice.com (visited June 8, 2006).

9. http://www.scamorama.com (visited June 8, 2006).

10. 18 U.S.C. § 2703(f).

11. South Carolina Code of Laws § 16-3-850. http://www.scstatehouse.net/CODE/t16c003.htm (visited June 8, 2006).

12. http://conventions.coe.int/Treaty/en/Treaties/Html/185.htm (visited July 7, 2006).

13. phoenix.fbi.gov/dojpressrel/2006/canspam013106.htm (visited June 9, 2006); www.usdoj.gov/criminal/press_room/press_releases/2006_4489_3-06-06ceosSpamClason.pdf (visited June 9, 2006).

14. *R v. Steven George Hourmouzis*, County Court, Melbourne (Stott, J.), October 30, 2000. http://www.countycourt.vic.gov.au/CA256D90000479B3/Lookup/Judgments_H/$file/hourmouz.pdf (visited June 8, 2006).

APPENDIX

USEFUL WEBSITES RELATING TO ELECTRONIC CRIME

Australian Institute of Criminology, Cybercrime Research
http://www.aic.gov.au/topics/cybercrime

Computer Crime Research Center (Ukraine)
http://www.crime-research.org

Cyberangels (United States)
http://www.cyberangels.org

Cyber-Rights and Cyber-Liberties (UK)
http://www.cyber-rights.org

Cybersecurity Resources
http://www.bna.com/webwatch/cybersecurityjanuary2006.htm

Dartmouth College, Institute for Information Infrastructure Protection
http://www.thei3p.org

Dorothy Denning's Home Page
http://www.cs.georgetown.edu/~denning

Electronic Crime Statistics
http://www.aic.gov.au/topics/cybercrime/stats/cybercrime.html
http://www.ojp.usdoj.gov/nij/topics/ecrime/welcome.html

Electronic Frontier Foundation
http://www.eff.org

Electronic Privacy Information Center
http://www.epic.org

European Union Forum on Cybercrime
http://cybercrime-forum.jrc.it/default

Examples of Hacked Web Pages
http://www.2600.com/hacked_pages/old_archives.html
(*Caution:* Readers are urged not to emulate the exploits depicted herein, as such a course of action is likely to entail the commission of a criminal offense.)

Gene Spafford's Home Page
http://homes.cerias.purdue.edu/%7Espaf/index.html

Harvard Law School, The Berkman Center for Internet and Society
http://cyber.law.harvard.edu/home

Infowar.Com
http://www.infowar.com

Internet Fraud Complaint Center
http://www.ifccfbi.gov/index.asp

Internet Watch Foundation (UK)
http://www.internetwatch.org.uk

Lawrence Lessig's Home Page
http://www.lessig.org

Netsafe (New Zealand)
http://www.netsafe.org.nz/home/home_default.aspx

Oxford Internet Institute
http://www.oii.ox.ac.uk

U.S. Department of Justice, Computer Crime and Intellectual Property Section
http://www.cybercrime.gov/index.html

U.S. Federal Bureau of Investigation, Cyber Investigations
http://www.fbi.gov/ipr

U.S. National Counter Intelligence Executive
http://www.nacic.gov/publications/law_policy/index.html

U.S. National Infrastructure Advisory Council
http://www.dhs.gov/dhspublic/interapp/editorial/editorial_0353.xml

U.S. President's Critical Infrastructure Protection Board
http://www.whitehouse.gov/pcipb

REFERENCES

Allen, J., S. Forrest, M. Levi, R. Hanna, M. Sutton, and D. Wilson. 2005. *Fraud and technology crimes: Findings from the 2002/03 British Crime Survey and 2003 Offending, Crime and Justice Survey*. London: Home Office. http://www.homeoffice.gov.uk/rds/pdfs05/rdsolr3405.pdf (visited June 9, 2006).

Ashcroft, John. 2004. *The Regpay child pornography indictment*. http://www.usdoj.gov/opa/pr/2004/January/04_ag_021.htm (visited June 9, 2006).

Associated Press. 1999. *Man guilty of Internet stalking*. http://www.bayinsider.com/news/1999/01/20/stalking.html (visited July 1, 1999).

AusCERT. 2006. *2006 Australian Computer Crime and Security Survey*. http://www.auscert.org.au/images/ACCSS2006.pdf (visited June 1, 2006).

Australian. 2005. Cannibal Meiwes to be retried. November 2. http://www.theaustralian.news.com.au/common/story_page/0,5744,17114357%255E1702,00.html (visited June 9, 2006).

BBC News. 2002. Online paedophile suspects arrested. August 28. http://news.bbc.co.uk/1/hi/wales/2220998.stm (visited June 8, 2006).

Beh, Hazel Glenn. 2001. Physical losses in cyberspace. *Connecticut Insurance Law Journal* 8:55–86.

Brenner, Susan, Brian Carrier, and Jef Henninger. 2004. The Trojan horse defense in cybercrime cases. *Santa Clara Computer and High Tech Law Journal* 21:1–53.

Business Software Alliance. 2005. *Second Annual BSA and IDC Global Software Piracy Study*. http://download.microsoft.com/download/F/0/3/F034C5EE-7E49-402A-9D5C-BD81C1D0AF94/IDC-Piracy%20Study.pdf (visited June 1, 2006).

Carnegie-Mellon Software Engineering Institute. 2005. *Cert Coordination Centre*. http://www.cert.org (visited June 9, 2006).

Casey, Eoghan. 2000. *Digital evidence and computer crime: Forensic science, computers and the Internet*. San Diego, Calif: Academic Press.

Cohen, L., and M. Felson. 1979. Social change and crime rate trends: A routine activity approach. *American Sociological Review* 44:588–608.

DeMarco, Joseph V. 2001. It's not just fun and "war games"—Juveniles and computer crime. *U.S. Attorneys Bulletin* 49, no. 3:48–55. http://www.usdoj.gov/criminal/cybercrime/usamay2001_7.htm (visited June 9, 2006).

Denning, Dorothy. 2001. Cyberwarriors: Activists and terrorists turn to cyberspace. *Harvard International Review* 23, no. 2:70–75.

Denning, Dorothy, and William E. Baugh, Jr. 2000. Hiding crimes in cyberspace. In *Cybercrime: Law enforcement, security and surveillance in the information age*, edited by Douglas Thomas and Brian D. Loader. London: Routledge.

Duva, Jason A. 1997. Online hacker pleads guilty to felony computer fraud. *Boston College Intellectual Property and Technology Forum*, 012301. http://www.bc.edu/bc_org/avp/law/st_org/iptf/headlines/content/1997012301.html (visited June 9, 2006).

Edwards, O. 1995. Hackers from hell. *Forbes*, October 9, 182.

Eichenwald, Kurt. 2005. Through his webcam, a boy joins a sordid online world. *New York Times*, December 19. http://www.nytimes.com/2005/12/19/national/19kids.ready .html?hp&ex=1135054800&en=5eb58e4d773204ee&ei=5094&partner=homepage (visited June 9, 2006).

Electronic Privacy Information Center. 2003. *United States v. Scarfo*, Criminal No. 00-404 (D.N.J.). http://www.epic.org/crypto/scarfo.html (visited June 9, 2006).

Electronic Privacy Information Center. 2005. *"Terrorism" Information Awareness (TIA)*. http://www.epic.org/privacy/profiling/tia (visited June 9, 2006).

Goodell, Jeff. 1996. *The cyberthief and the samurai*. New York: Dell.

Goodman, Marc. 1997. Why the police don't care about computer crime. *Harvard Journal of Law and Technology*, 10, no. 3:465–494.

Goodman, Marc. 2001. Making computer crime count. *FBI Law Enforcement Bulletin*, August. http://www.fbi.gov/publications/leb/2001/august2001/aug01p10.htm (visited June 9, 2006).

Gordon, Gary R., Chet Hosmer, Christine Siedsma, and Don Rebovich. 2002. *Assessing technology, methods, and information for committing and combating cybercrime*. Washington, D.C.: U.S. Department of Justice.

Gordon, Lawrence A., Martin P. Loeb, William Lucyshyn, and Robert Richardson. 2005. *2005 CSI/FBI Computer Crime and Security Survey*. http://www.cybercrime.gov/ FBI2005.pdf (visited June 9, 2006).

Grabosky, Peter, and Russell G. Smith. 1998. *Crime in the digital age*. Sydney and New Brunswick, N.J.: Federation Press/Transaction.

Grabosky, Peter, Russell G. Smith, and Gillian Dempsey. 2001. *Electronic theft: Unlawful acquisition in cyberspace*. Cambridge, England: Cambridge University Press.

Grant, Anna, Fiona David, and Peter Grabosky. 2001. The commercial sexual exploitation of children. *Current Issues in Criminal Justice*, 12, no. 3:269–287.

Grossman, Lev. 2000. Attack of the Love Bug. *Time*, May 15, 49.

Hafner, Katie, and John Markoff. 1991. *Cyberpunk: Outlaws and hackers on the electronic frontier*. New York: Simon & Schuster.

Hansell, Saul. 2004. *When software fails to stop spam, it's time to bring in the detectives*. http://select.nytimes.com/gst/abstract.html?res=FA0A14FB345A0C728FDDAC0894 DC404482 (visited June 9, 2006).

Hyde-Bales, Kathryn, Sheridan Morris, and Andrew Charlton. 2004. *The police recording of computer crime*. London: Home Office. http://www.homeoffice.gov.uk/ rds/pdfs04/dpr40.pdf (visited June 9, 2006).

Kay, Russell. 2005. Quick study: Biometric authentication. *Computerworld*, April 4. http://www.computerworld.com/securitytopics/security/story/0,10801,100772,00. html (visited June 9, 2006).

Keelty, Mick. 2004. *The dark side of technology*. Presented to a Conference of the Australian Institute of Criminology, November 29, Melbourne. http://www. aic.gov.au/conferences/2004/keelty.html (visited June 9, 2006).

Koops, Bert-Jaap, and Susan W. Brenner (eds.) 2006. *Cybercrime and jurisdiction: A global survey*. The Hague: T.M.C. Asser Press.

Kowalski, Melanie. 2002. *Cyber-crime: Issues, data sources and feasibility of collecting police-reported statistics*. Ottawa: Statistics Canada. http://dsp-psd.pwgsc.gc.ca/ Collection/Statcan/85-558-X/85-558-XIE2002001.pdf (visited June 9, 2006).

Krone, T. 2005a. *Phishing*. High Tech Crime Brief No. 9. Canberra: Australian Institute of Criminology. http://www.aic.gov.au/publications/htcb/htcb009.html (visited June 9, 2006).

Krone, T. 2005b. Queensland police stings in online chat rooms. *Trends and Issues in Crime and Criminal Justice*, no. 301. Canberra: Australian Institute of Criminology. http://www.aic.gov.au/publications/tandi2/tandi301.html (visited June 9, 2006).

Levy, Steven. 1984. *Hackers: Heroes of the computer revolution*. New York: Penguin Books.

Liptak, Adam. 2006. In case about Google's secrets, yours are safe. *New York Times*, January 26. http://www.nytimes.com/2006/01/26/technology/26privacy.html?emc= eta1 (visited June 9, 2006).

Magee, John F. 2003. The law regulating unsolicited commercial e-mail: An international perspective. *Santa Clara Computer and High-Technology Law Journal* 19, no. 2: 333.

Malcolm, John G. 2002. Paper presented to Special Briefing: Money Laundering and Payment Systems in Online Gambling, sponsored by World Online Gambling Law Report, November 20, London. http://www.usdoj.gov/criminal/cybercrime/ JGM_Intgambling.htm (visited June 9, 2006).

Mazerolle, Lorraine, and Janet Ransley. 2006. *Third party policing*. Cambridge, England: Cambridge University Press.

McCullagh, Declan. (2006a). Gonzales pressures ISPs on data retention. ZDNet News. May 26, 2006, 5:29 PM PT. http://news.zdnet.com/2100-1009_22-6077654.html (visited June 13, 2006).

McCullagh, Declan. (2006b). Congress may consider mandatory ISP snooping. ZDNet News. April 28, 2006, 5:06 PM PT. http://news.zdnet.com/2100-9588_22- 6066608.html?tag=nl (visited June 13, 2006).

McCusker, R. 2005. Spam: Nuisance or menace, prevention or cure? *Trends and Issues in Crime and Criminal Justice*, no. 294. Canberra: Australian Institute of Criminology. http://www.aic.gov.au/publications/tandi2/tandi294.pdf (visited June 9, 2006).

McKemmish, Rodney. 1999. What is forensic computing? *Trends and Issues in Crime and Criminal Justice*, no. 118. Canberra: Australian Institute of Criminology. http://www.aic.gov.au/publications/tandi/ti118.pdf (visited June 9, 2006).

McNicol, Tony. 2005. Cyber war grips Asia. *Japan Times Online*, June 14. http:// www.japantimes.co.jp/cgi-bin/getarticle.pl5?fl20050614zg.htm (visited June 9, 2006).

Miller, Greg, and Davan Maharaj. 1999. N. Hollywood man charged in 1st cyber-stalking case. *Los Angeles Times*, January 22. http://www.cs.csubak.edu/~donna/news/ crime.html#stalking (visited June 9, 2006).

Mitnick, Kevin D. 2002. *The art of deception: Controlling the human element of security*. Indianapolis, Ind.: Wiley.

Morris, Sheridan. 2004. The future of Netcrime now. Home Office Online Report 62/04. Home Office, London. http://www.homeoffice.gov.uk/rds/pdfs04/rdsolr6204.pdf (visited July 25, 2006).

Morton, Tom. 2004. *Mutating mobiles*. Background Briefing, ABC Radio National, April 25. http://www.abc.net.au/rn/talks/bbing/stories/s1096804.htm (visited June 9, 2006).

Motion Picture Association. 2003a. *Motion Picture Association (MPA) announces expeditious resolution of two landmark civil action proceedings concerning DVD piracy in China*. Encino, Calif./Hong Kong: MPA.

Motion Picture Association. 2003b. *Motion Picture Association (MPA) announces the successful resolution of six civil action proceedings concerning DVD piracy in Shanghai.* Encino, Calif./Hong Kong: MPA.

Nasheri, Hedieh. 2005. *Corporate espionage and industrial spying.* Cambridge, England: Cambridge University Press.

Neumann, Peter G. 1996. CIA disconnects home page after being hacked. *Risks Digest* 18 (September 25), 49. http://catless.ncl.ac.uk/Risks/18.49.html#subj2 (visited June 9, 2006).

Newman, Graeme R., and Ronald V. Clarke. 2003. *Superhighway robbery: Preventing e-commerce crime.* Devon, England: Willan Publishing.

New York Times. 2005. Sydney violence fueled by race, ignorance and youth. December 15. http://www.nytimes.com/reuters/international/international-australia-beach-violence.html (visited June 9, 2006).

Ogilvie, Emma. 2000. Cyberstalking. *Trends and Issues in Crime and Criminal Justice,* no. 166, Australian Institute of Criminology, Canberra. http://www.aic.gov.au/publications/tandi/tandi166.html (visited June 1, 2006).

Orwell, George. 1951. *Nineteen eighty-four.* London: Secker & Warburg.

Painter, Christopher. 2001. Supervised release and probation restrictions in hacker cases. *U.S. Attorneys Bulletin* 49:2.

Parker, Donn B. 1976. *Crime by computer.* New York: Charles Scribner's Sons.

Pontell, Henry N., and Stephen M. Rosoff. 2005. *White-collar delinquency.* Unpublished manuscript. Department of Criminology Law and Society, University of California, Irvine.

Power, Richard. 2000. *Tangled web: Tales of digital crime from the shadows of cyberspace.* Indianapolis, Ind.: Que Publishers.

Rheingold, Howard. 2002. *Smart mobs: The next social revolution.* Cambridge, Mass.: Perseus Books.

Richtel, Matt. 2005. Live tracking of mobile phones prompts court fights on privacy. *New York Times,* December 10. http://www.nytimes.com/2005/12/10/technology/10phone.html?ex=1291870800&en=2011ce3dd6b43183&ei=5088&partner=rssnyt&emc=rss (visited June 12, 2006).

Risen, James, and Eric Lichtblau. 2005. Bush lets U.S. spy on callers without courts. *New York Times,* December 16, 1.

Rosoff, Stephen M., Henry N. Pontell, and Robert H. Tillman. 1998. *Profit without honor: White-collar crime and the looting of America.* Upper Saddle River, N.J.: Prentice Hall.

Rustad, Michael. 2001. Private enforcement of cybercrime on the electronic frontier. *Southern California Interdisciplinary Law Journal* 11, no. 1:63–116.

Schiesel, Seth. 2004. Turning the tables on e-mail swindlers. *New York Times,* June 17. http://www.nytimes.com/2004/06/17/technology/circuits/17hoax.html?ex=1402891200&en=c41168a8fa42945f&ei=5007&partner=USERLAND (visited June 9, 2006).

Schneider, Jacqueline. 2003. Hiding in plain sight: An exploration of the illegal(?) activities of a drugs newsgroup. *Howard Journal,* 42, no. 4:374–389.

Seltzer, William, and Margo Anderson. 2001. The dark side of numbers: The role of population data systems in human rights abuses. *Social Research* 68, no. 2:481–514.

Sieber, U. 1998. *Legal aspects of computer-related crime in the information society.* COMCRIME study prepared for the European Commission. http://europa.eu.int/ISPO/legal/en/comcrime/sieber.doc (visited June 9, 2006).

Slatalla, Michelle, and Joshua Quittner. 1995. *Masters of deception: The gang that ruled cyberspace.* New York: Harper Collins.

Smith, Russell G., Peter Grabosky, and Gregor Urbas. 2004. *Cybercriminals on trial.* Cambridge, England: Cambridge University Press.

Sorkin, David E. 2001. Technical and legal approaches to unsolicited electronic mail. *University of San Francisco Law Review* 35:325.

Sterling, Bruce. 1992. *The hacker crackdown.* New York: Bantam Books.

Stoll, Clifford. 1989. *The cuckoo's egg.* New York: Pocket Books.

Sussmann, Michael A. 1999. The critical challenges from international high tech and computer related crime at the millennium. *Duke Journal of Comparative and International Law* 9:451–489.

Thomas, Douglas, and Brian D. Loader (eds.). 2000. *Cybercrime.* London: Routledge.

Thomas, T.L. 2003. Al Qaeda and the Internet: The danger of "cyberplanning." *Parameters* 33, no. 1:112–123. http://carlisle-www.army.mil/usawc/Parameters/03spring/thomas.htm (visited June 1, 2006).

Thompson, Clive. 2004. The virus underground. *New York Times Magazine,* February 8. http://engineering.dartmouth.edu/~engs004/virusarticle.html (visited June 9, 2006).

United Kingdom, Biometrics Working Group. 2006. *Use of biometrics for identification: Advice on product selection.* http://www.cesg.gov.uk/site/ast/biometrics/media/BiometricsAdvice.pdf (visited June 12, 2006).

U.S. Attorney's Office, Middle District of Georgia. 2005. Press release, March 23. http://www.usdoj.gov/usao/gam/press_releases/2005/050323_okeefe.html (visited June 9, 2006).

U.S. Department of Justice. 1998. *Israeli citizen arrested in Israel for hacking United States and Israeli government computers.* Press release, March 18. http://www.usdoj.gov/criminal/cybercrime/ehudpr.htm (visited June 9, 2006).

U.S. Department of Justice. 2001a. *Three men indicted for shill bidding ring that auctioned fake Diebenkorn painting for $135,805.* Press release, March 8. http://www.usdoj.gov/criminal/cybercrime/Fetterman_indict.htm (visited December 20, 2005); *United States v. Fetterman* (Plea Agreement of Scott Beach) (E.D. Cal. April 17, 2001). http://www.usdoj.gov/criminal/cybercrime/ebaypleaagree.pdf (visited June 9, 2006).

U.S. Department of Justice. 2001b. *Computer security expert sentenced to 27 months' imprisonment for computer hacking and electronic eavesdropping.* Press release, June 13. http://www.cybercrime.gov/OquendoSent.htm (visited June 9, 2006).

U.S. Department of Justice. 2002a. *Six defendants sentenced in $16 million bogus investment scheme marketed over Internet.* Press release, January 30. http://www.usdoj.gov/criminal/cybercrime/guastella_martins.htm (visited June 9, 2006).

U.S. Department of Justice. 2002b. *Searching and seizing computers and obtaining electronic evidence in criminal investigations.* Washington, D.C.: U.S. Department of Justice. http://www.usdoj.gov/criminal/cybercrime/s&smanual2002.htm (visited June 9, 2006).

U.S. Department of Justice. 2003. *Defendant indicted in connection with operating illegal Internet software piracy group.* Press release, March 12. http://www.usdoj. gov/criminal/cybercrime/griffithsIndict.htm (visited June 9, 2006).

U.S. Department of Justice. 2004a. *Six Internet fradusters indicted in international conspiracy to steal more than $10 million from world's largest technology distributor.* Press release, August 4. http://www.usdoj.gov/criminal/cybercrime/mateiasIndict.htm (visited June 9, 2006).

U.S. Department of Justice. 2004b. *Former employee of a Massachusetts high-technology firm charged with computer hacking.* Press release, August 23. http://www.usdoj. gov/criminal/cybercrime/angleCharged.htm (visited June 9, 2006).

U.S. Department of Justice. 2004c. *Hacker sentenced to prison for breaking into Lowe's Companies' computers with intent to steal credit card information.* Press release, December 15. http://www.usdoj.gov/criminal/cybercrime/salcedoSent.htm (visited June 9, 2006).

U.S. Department of Justice. 2005a. *Creator and four users of Loverspy spyware program indicted.* Press release, August 26. http://www.cybercrime.gov/perezIndict.htm (visited June 9, 2006).

U.S. Department of Justice. 2005b. *Justice Department announces conviction of Florida man accused of massive data theft from Acxiom, Inc.* Press release, August 12. http://www.usdoj.gov/criminal/cybercrime/levineConvict.htm (visited June 9, 2006).

U.S. Department of Justice. 2005c. *Disgruntled Phillies fan/spammer sent to prison for four years.* Press release, July 14. http://www.usdoj.gov/criminal/cybercrime/ carlsonSent.htm (visited June 9, 2006).

U.S. Department of Justice. 2005d. *Massachusetts teen convicted for hacking into Internet and telephone service providers and making bomb threats to high schools in Massachusetts and Florida.* Press release, September 8. http://www.cybercrime.gov/ juvenileSentboston.htm (visited June 9, 2006).

U.S. Department of Justice. 2005e. *Operation Buccaneer.* http://www.usdoj.gov/criminal/ cybercrime/ob/OBMain.htm (visited June 9, 2006).

U.S. Federal Bureau of Investigation. 2003. *Carnivore/DCS-1000 report to Congress.* http://www.epic.org/privacy/carnivore/2003_report.pdf (visited June 9, 2006).

U.S. General Accounting Office. 2004. *Data mining: Federal efforts cover a wide range of uses.* Washington, D.C.: U.S. Government Accounting Office. http://www.gao.gov/ new.times/d04548.pdf (visited June 8, 2006).

U.S. Securities and Exchange Commission. 2000. *In the Matter of Jonathan G. Lebed.* http://www.sec.gov/litigation/admin/33-7891.htm (visited June 9, 2006).

Vaughan, Diane. 1983. *Controlling unlawful organizational behavior: Social structure and corporate misconduct.* Chicago: University of Chicago Press.

Warren, Samuel, and Louis Brandeis. 1890. The right to privacy. *Harvard Law Review* 4, no. 5:193–220.

White House. 2003. *The national strategy to secure cyberspace.* Washington: White House. http://www.whitehouse.gov/pcipb/ (visited June 9, 2006).

Wible, Brent. 2003. A site where hackers are welcome: Using hack-in contests to shape preferences and deter computer crime. *Yale Law Journal* 112:1577–1623.

Wilson, Clay. 2005. *Computer attack and cyberterrorism: Vulnerabilities and policy issues for Congress.* Washington, D.C.: Congressional Research Service, Library of Congress. http://fpc.state.gov/documents/organization/45184.pdf (visited June 9, 2006).

INDEX

A

Access codes, 14–15
Access to computers, 44–45
  control strategies, 94
Addiction to computers (as defense), 80
Advance-fee fraud letters, 30, 31–32
  nonreporting of, 49–50
  private citizens' actions, 99–100
America Online
  criminal warrants, 67
Anonymous e-mail, 13
Antivirus software, 28
Ardita, Julio César ("Gritón"), 15–16
ATM fraud, 24–25, 103
Auctions online
  complaints, 52–53
  fraud, 23
  security enforcement, 96–97
Australian High Tech Crime Centre
  (AHTCC), 79
Australian Institute of Criminology,
  52, 66

B

Backups, double copies of, 71
Bill of Rights (U.S.), 100
Biometric authentication, techniques
  listed, 94
Blue boxes, 20
Bot (abbreviation of robot)
  definition, 13
  in denial of service attacks, 29
Botnets, 50
Brandeis, Louis, 64
British Crime Survey (BCS), 53
Bush, George W., 67
Business Software Alliance, 53

C

Calling card number theft, 21
CAN SPAM Act (2003), 104
Canada, 29, 39
Carnivore (DCS 1000) network collection
  technologies, 67
Casinos, online, 34
Categories of computer crime, 11–14

Celebrity (or notoriety) motive, 45
Cellular phones, 17–18
Center for Online and Internet
  Addiction, 80
Child pornography
  background, 12, 14
  commercialization, 59
  defenses, 80, 81
  evidence of knowledge and
    intent, 81
  fantasy defense, 82
  legislation, 8
  motives, 45
  offensive content, 34
  online investigations, 73
  Operation Artus, 78
  Operation Cathedral, 77–78
  Operation Falcon, 78–79
  private citizens against, 99
  requirement to assist governments,
    100–102
  sentencing, 27, 84
China, 97
CIA (Central Intelligence Agency), 25
Civil remedies, 97
  spam violations, 104
Civility, culture of cyberspace, 92
Code Red Virus, 58
Commercialization, 59–60
Competition, 26
Computer Emergency Readiness Team
  (US—CERT), 98
Computer Emergency Response Team
  (CERT), 97–98
Computer Fraud and Abuse Act, 16
Computer Security Institute, 52
Computer-mediated communications,
  illegal interception of, 17–18
Computer-related crime. See
  Electronic crime
Computers
  as instruments, 11
  as targets, 11
Conspiracies, criminal, 18–20
Content regulation, 8, 9
  problems with, 34–35

Copyright protection
  Operation Buccaneer, 78
  piracy and, 35
  security enforcement and, 97
Corporate fraud
  information systems and, 6
Corporate intelligence collection, 26
Costs of computer crime, 51
Council of Europe Cybercrime
      Convention, 103, 105
Counter-hackers, 99
Counter-scammers, 99–100
Counterfeiting. *See also* Websites,
      counterfeiting
  prosecution, 86
  scanning technology, 36
Crackers, 6
Credit cards
  online fraud, 53
  theft of card details, 26–27
  wireless technology, 27
Crime in the Digital Age (Grabosky
      and Smith), 3
Crime scenes, 70
Criminal havens, 57
Criminal procedure, law of
  adaptation of, 102
  challenges of networked
      environments, 8
Critical infrastructure
  attacks against, 38–40
  as opportunity for crime, 46
Cryptography, 63–64
Cuckoo's Egg, The (Stoll), 16
Cyber Angels, 99
Cyber watchdog, 99
Cyber-extortion, 32–33
Cybercrime. *See also* Electronic crime
  basic trends, 58–61
  commercialization, 59–60
  cryptography, 63–64
  integration, 60–61
  juvenile involvement, 61–63
  sophistication, 58–59
  three factors, 43
  use of term, 2
Cyberterrorism, 38
Cybervigilantes, 98–102

D
"Dark figure" offenses, 49
Data
  destruction or damage to, 25

Data processing technology, 5–6
Data theft, 26–27
Data-matching technologies, 65
"Datastream Cowboy," 16–17
Day trading, 23
Defense Advanced Research Projects
      Agency (DARPA), 66–67
Defenses, 80–82
Denial-of-service attacks, 28–29
  as dramatic crime, 14
  juvenile case, 62
  losses from, 52
  Port of Houston, 40
Department of Homeland Security, 98
Digital divide
  use of term, 57
Digital technology
  disadvantages, 1–2
  research uses of, 1
  restrictions on offenders, 87–89
Direct Marketing Association, 96
Disadvantages of digital technology, 1–2
Distributed denial-of-service attacks, 29
  defense, 80–81
  definition, 12
Drink or Die piracy group, 35
Drug trafficking
  as computer-related crime, 51
Dumpster diving, 14

E
E-commerce
  complaints since 1998, 53
  costs of crime, 55
  increasing volume of, 46
  losses to, 51
  online credit card fraud, 53
  privacy threats, 65
  spam and, 105
E-mail. *See also* Spam (unsolicited
      commercial e-mail)
  anonymous, 13
  invitation to check out website, 37–38
  legislation, 104
  misadventures with, 50
  phishing, 37–38
E-mail addresses, sale of, 50
Eavesdropping, electronic, 72
Economic intelligence, 26
Electronic crime
  future of, 105–107
  use of term, 2
Electronic criminal havens, 57

Embezzlement
    computer use in, 5–6
    fraud, 24
Encryption
    credit card details, 26
    in criminal conspiracies, 18–19
    definition, 13
    described, 18
    security uses, 48
    trends, 63
Encryption key
    loss of data, 25
    managing encrypted evidence, 72
Equity Funding scandal, 6
Espionage, 26
Etiquette, 92
European Commission on Human
        Rights, 64
Evidence, digital
    basic issues, 74–75
    principles for handling, 73–74
Extortion, 32–33
    background, 12
    cyber-extortion, 32–33
    means used, 51
Eye scan techniques, 94

F

Facial recognition techniques, 94
Falun Gong, 34
Fantasy defense, 82
FBI (Federal Bureau of Investigation)
    Carnivore data collection, 67
    Computer Analysis Response Team
        (CART), 74
    key logger system, 72
    survey, 52
Federal Guidelines for Searching and
        Seizing Computers (1994), 74
Fifth Amendment, 63–64
Financial crimes
    Internet phishing, 50
    motives, 45
    trends, 54
Fingerprint scanners, 94
First Law of Electronic Crime, 106
Foreign prosecution, 106
Forensic computing specialists,
        private, 70
Forensic practices, standardizing,
        74–75
Forgery, 36
Fourth Amendment, 71–73

Fraud, 21–25
    ATM fraud, 24–25, 103
    auction fraud, 23
    embezzlement, 24
    fraudulent ordering of goods, 22
    manipulation of stock prices, 22–23
    sales and investment fraud, 21–22
    technology-neutral language
        of laws, 103
    unauthorized funds transfer, 23–24

G

Gambling, online facilities, 34
Global positioning technology, 17, 19
Global reach of electronic crime, 2
Goods, fraudulent ordering of, 22
Google research tools
    example of, 66
Google search engines
    Internet pornography law, 68
Government
    Carnivore (DCS 1000) network
        collection technologies, 67
    privacy threats by, 65–68
    role of, 102
Guardians, absence of capable, 47–48
Guardianship strategies, 94–95
Guilty pleas, 79–80

H

Hacker Crackdown, The (Sterling), 6
Hacker culture
    strategies to change, 92–93
"Hacker-for-hire," 60
Hackers
    celebrity status, 15–17
    folk-hero status of, 6
    mobile hackers, 58
    Phone Masters, 21
    Romanian online ordering, 22
    use of term, 6
Hacking, 14–17
    automated tools for, 15, 58
    counter-hacker, 99
    definition, 12
    exemplary prosecutions, 82–83
    intelligent malware, 58
    motives, 45
    special skills enhancement and
        sentencing, 85–87
    use of term, 14
Hand geometry, 94
Happy Hardcore, 20–21

Hardening the target
  banks, 70
  measures, 46–47
  new technologies of access control, 94
Health insurance fraud, 6
History of electronic crime
      legislation, 7–9
History of electronic offending, 5–7

I

Illegal interception, 17–18
ILOVEYOU virus, 27, 54, 55
  legislation, 102, 105
Impacts of cybercrime, 54–55
Incidence of crime, 50–51
Incidental to offense, computer as, 11
Instrument, computer as, 11
Integration, 60–61
Intellectual property rights
  legislation, 8
  piracy, 35, 84, 97
Intelligent malware, 58
International cooperation, 103
  Council of Europe Cybercrime
      Convention, 103, 105
  foreign prosecution, 106
  G8 plan, 105
International Organization on Computer
      Evidence (IOCE), 74
Internet
  extreme relationships, 19–20
  pedophile solicitations, 19
  revolution in high-tech crime, 6
  world regions by usage and
      population, 44–45
Internet Fraud Complaint Center
      (IFCC), 52
Internet relay chat (IRC), 78
Internet safety groups, 99
Internet service provider (ISP)
  data retention policies, 75
  illegal use of services, 20
  law enforcement and, 75, 96
  requirements to assist governments, 100
  spam control, 96
  theft, 20–21
Investigation, 69–79
  adapting techniques to cyberspace, 102
Investment solicitations, fraudulent,
      21–22, 30–32
  Nigerian advance-fee fraud letter, 30,
      31–32
Islamic nations, 34

J

Junk faxes, 105
Jurisdictional issues, 76–77
Juvenile involvement, 61–63
  See also Mafiaboy

K

Key logger system (KLS), 72
Key loggers
  definition, 13
"Kuji," 16–17

L

Law enforcement
  data retention, 75
"Legion of Doom," 17
Legislation, 102–105
  e-mail, 104
  history of, 7–9
Levin, Vladimir, 24
Loverspy program, 18

M

"Mafiaboy," 29, 39
  costs of attacks, 55
Mail bombing, 29
  of critical infrastructure, 38
Malicious code, 27–28
  commercialization, 60
  definition, 13
  as dramatic crime, 14
  impact of, 54
  sophistication, 58
  in spam, 60–61
Malware, 81
"Masters of Deception," 17
Melissa virus, 28, 55
Misadventures, innocent explanations
      for, 50
Mitnick, Kevin
  offenses listed, 16
  postrelease restrictions
      on, 87–89
Mobile hackers, 58
Mobile phone technology, 17–18
Money laundering, 33–34
Morris, Robert, 7
Morris worm, 97
Motion Picture Association
      DVD piracy, 97
Motives for electronic
      crime, 44–45
  strategies, 92–93

N

National security
  data theft, 26
Nature of investigations, 70
Neo-Nazi propaganda, 34
Netsafe, 95
Network scanning program
  definition, 13
New technologies
  impact of, 1
Nigerian advance-fee fraud letter,
  30, 31–32
  nonreporting of, 49–50
NIMDA virus, 58
Nonreporting, 49

O

Obscene telephone calls, 36
Offensive content, 34–35
  complaints, 53
  regulation, 8
Online banking
  money laundering, 33
Operation Artus, 78
Operation Buccaneer, 78
Operation Cathedral, 77–78
Operation Cybersnare, 73
Operation Falcon, 78–79
Opportunity
  defense strategies, 93–94

P

Palm geometry, 94
Password crackers
  definition, 13
Passwords, 14–15
Pedophiles, 19
Personal computer, significance of, 6
Phishing, 37–38
  botnets, 60
  definition, 12
  sophistication, 59
Phone Masters hacker group, 21
Phone phreakers, 20
Phreaking, 5
  low-tech alternative, 20
Piracy, 35
  civil remedies, 97
  music and video, 97
  nations with highest and lowest
    rates, 53
  Operation Buccaneer, 78
  sentencing, 84

Police
  computer crime and, 50–51
  investigation interests, 70
Political communications, 105
Pornography law, 68
Privacy threats, 64–68
  protective legislation, 7
  sources of, 65
  from the state, 65–68
Private citizens, 98–102
Private enforcement, 96–98
Programmers, falsification of data, 5
Proportionate sentencing, 83
Prosecution, 79–83
  defenses, 80–82
  exemplary prosecutions, 82–83
  foreign, 106
Psychological warfare, 41

R

Reasons for electronic crime
  guardians, 47–48
  motives, 44–45
  opportunities, 46–47
  theoretical frameworks, 43
Rebellion motive, 45
Recording Industry Association of
  America (RIAA), 97
Remote search technologies, 72
Reno, Janet, 83
Revenge motive, 45
Rootkit, definition, 13
Routine activity theory, 43–48
  strategies listed, 91–95
Rule of law, 102–103

S

Sales and investment fraud, 21–22
Santayana, George, 107
Scanning technology and forgery, 36
Scholarship on electronic crime, 3
Search and seizure, 71–73
  anti-crime activities of private
    citizens, 100
Security, information
  capable guardianship, 95
  defense strategies, 93–94
  early attitudes to, 48
  New Zealand, 95
  pluralistic prevention, 95–96
  private enforcement, 96–98
Security law
  legislation citing threat of terrorism, 8

Security solutions software, 96
Sentencing, 83–89
    aims of punishment, 83
    child pornography, 27, 84
    encryption offenses in Europe
      and Australia, 64
    hackers, 27
    juveniles, 39, 52
    piracy, 84
    proportionate, 83
    restrictions on probation
      or parole, 87
    special skills enhancement, 85–87
    U.S. Sentencing Commission, 84
Sex slavery, 66
Signature dynamics, 94
Social engineering, 14–15
Sophistication of cybercrime, 58–59
South Carolina Criminal Code,
    100, 102
Spam (unsolicited commercial e-mail),
    29–32
    botnets, 60
    definition, 11
    investigations of, 96
    legislation, 9, 104–105
    malicious code in, 60–61
    privacy threats, 65
Special skills enhancement, 85–87
Spoofing, definition, 13
Spyware, 18
    stalking with, 37
Stalking, 36–37
    background, 14
    jurisdictional issues, 76
Statistics, 52–54
Steganography
    in criminal conspiracies, 18
    definition, 13
Steve Jackson Games, Inc. v. United States
    Secret Service (1994), 71
Stock prices
    day trading, 23
    manipulation of, 22–23
Stoll, Clifford, 16
Substantive criminal law, 102–103
System integrity, 93
System security
    as opportunity reduction, 46–47

T

Target of offense, computer as, 11
Target-hardening measures, 46–47, 70

Targets or prospective victims, 46–47
Telecom Australia (Telstra), 3
Telecommunications technology, 5
    law enforcement and, 75
Telegraph, 5
Telemarketing fraud, 5
Telephone, 5
    illegal use of services, 20
    obscene telephone calls, 36
Terrorism, 38
    legislation citing threat of, 8
    technology as means to facilitate,
      40–41
Terrorism Information Awareness
    Program, 66–67
Text messages
    to organize criminal activity, 19
Theft of data, 26–27
    espionage, 26
    theft of credit card details, 26–27
Theft of services, 20–21
Total Information Awareness
    Program, 66–67
Trade secrets, 26
Transnational cybercrime cases, 77
Trojan Horse
    to catch child pornographer, 101
    definition, 13
    Port of Houston defense, 40
    stalking with, 37
    surveys reporting, 54
Trojan Horse defense, 80–81
Types of cybercriminals, 69
Typing patterns, 94

U

Unauthorized access
    commercialization, 60
    defenses, 80
    as initial indicium, 59
    juvenile case, 62
    legislation, 7–8
    losses from, 52
    "new" crimes, 14
Unauthorized funds transfer, 23–24
United Kingdom
    Association of Chief Police
      Officers, 74–75
United Kingdom Biometrics Working
    Group, 94
United States v. Booker (2005), 84
United States v. Triumph Capital
    Group (2002), 74

U.S. Department of Justice, 68
    Computer Crime and Intellectual
        Property Section, 74
    data retention by ISPs, 75
U.S. Secret Service, 39
U.S. Sentencing Commission, 84
USA Patriot Act (Public Law 107-56), 8

V

Victimization surveys, 52
Virus, 26–27
    complaints, 53
    cost of, 54, 55
    definition, 12
    ILOVEYOU virus, 27, 54, 55, 102, 103
    losses from, 52
    scanners to combat, 93
    sophistication, 58
    speed of, 58
    surveys reporting, 54
Voice recognition techniques, 94

W

War driving, 58
Website defacement, 25
Websites
    counterfeiting, 36, 59,
        86–87
White-collar delinquency, 63
Wireless access points ("hot
    spots"), 58
Wireless local area networks
    (LANs), 58
Wireless technology, 58
    credit card details, 27
Wiretapping, 72
Worms, 27–28
    definition, 12
    first, 7
    joint investigations, 96
    Morris worm response,
        97–98
    surveys reporting, 54